D1259820

INTRODUCTION TO ECONOMIC HISTORY 1750–1950

By the same author

*

A HISTORY OF SOCIALIST THOUGHT
Vols. I–V

ATTEMPTS AT GENERAL UNION
A Study in British Trade Union History 1818–34

CHARTIST PORTRAITS

THE CASE FOR INDUSTRIAL PARTNERSHIP

With A. W. Filson

BRITISH WORKING CLASS MOVEMENTS
Select Documents 1789–1875

INTRODUCTION TO ECONOMIC HISTORY 1750-1950

BY

G. D. H. COLE

MACMILLAN
London · Melbourne · Toronto

ST MARTIN'S PRESS
New York
1967

—

First Edition 1952
Reprinted 1952, 1953, 1954, 1960, 1965, 1966, 1967

MACMILLAN AND COMPANY LIMITED
Little Essex Street London WC 2
also Bombay Calcutta Madras Melbourne

THE MACMILLAN COMPANY OF CANADA LIMITED
70 Bond Street Toronto 2

ST MARTIN'S PRESS INC
175 Fifth Avenue New York NY 10010

PRINTED IN GREAT BRITAIN

PREFACE

THIS volume, small though it is, has a long history. I wrote the first draft of it twenty years ago, with the intention of including it in my *Intelligent Man's Guide Through World Chaos*, but only a small section of it was finally used in that book, and several times since I have done a little work on it with the intention of publishing it separately. During the past year I have rewritten it, so that only a very little of my draft of twenty years ago survives. I have, however, to thank Mr. Victor Gollancz and Mr. Alfred Knopf, who published my *Intelligent Man's Guide* in Great Britain and in the United States, for permission to make use of the small part of it which did finally appear in that work. By far the greater part of the present volume is new: I make no claim that it is more than a very elementary introduction to a wide subject. My reason for publishing it is that, as far as I know, no similar brief introduction exists.

G. D. H. C.

OXFORD
March 1952

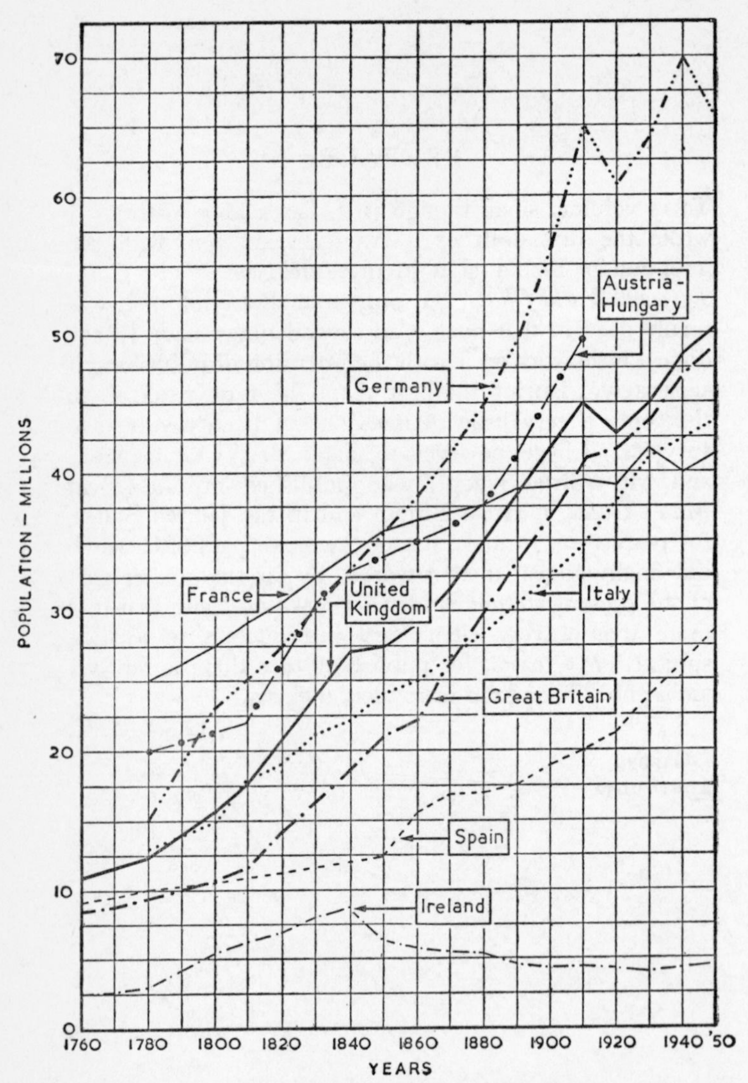

CHART 1: Rise of Population in Western and Central Europe, 1760-1950

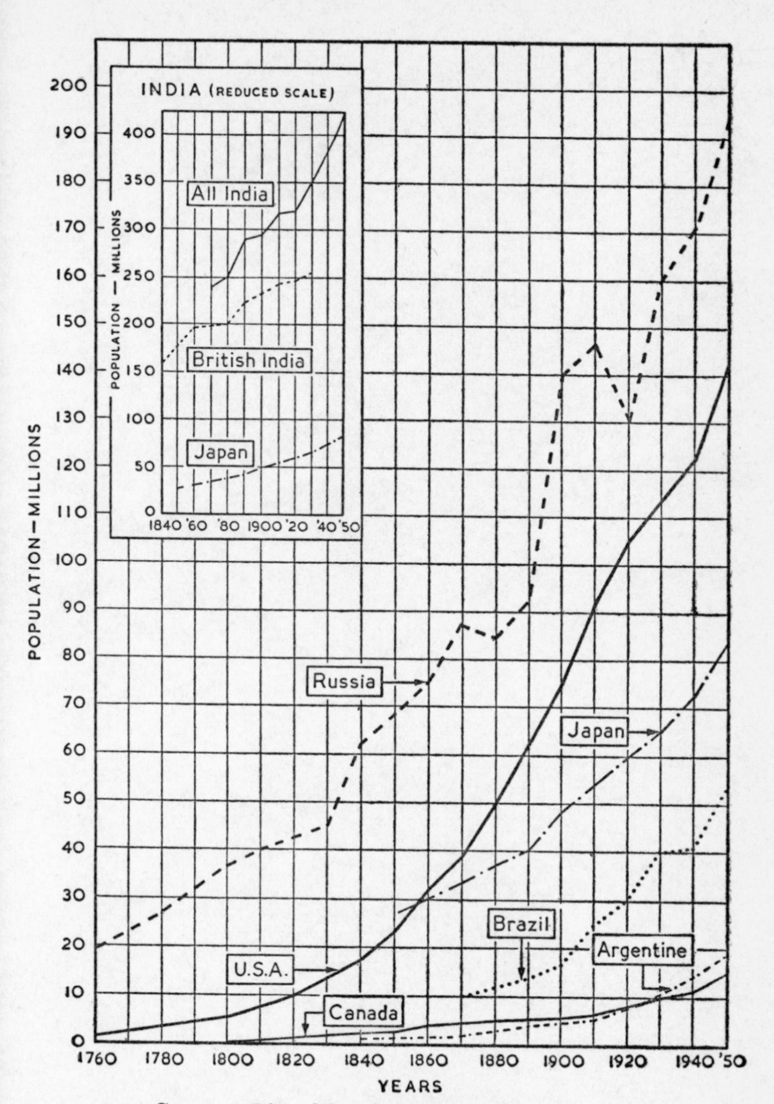

CHART 2: Rise of Population in Russia and in certain non-European Countries, 1760-1950

CONTENTS

CHARTS, MAP AND TABLES

I
Introductory

THIS short book can be only a most summary introduction to its subject. It is meant, not for economic historians, but for students of the modern world who want to have a general notion of the economic changes which, over the past two centuries, have transformed the entire way of living for a large section of the world's peoples and are to-day spreading to areas which had been little affected by them only a few years ago. How have these changes come about, and by what stages have they carried the world to its present condition? What lessons that will help to guide us in facing the future can we learn from what has happened hitherto?

To-day, in the countries which have been the principal centres of industrial development, most of the people live in towns, and the proportion living in the countryside shows a continuous tendency to fall. After a period of rapidly rising populations, most of these countries have experienced a sharp fall in their birth-rates, which the continual fall in infant mortality and the longer expectation of life have not sufficed to counteract. Their populations are now, for the most part, increasing but slowly, and in some cases not at all; but there is a steady tendency for the age-composition to alter, with fewer children being born and more men and women surviving into old age. Town-dwelling has greatly altered the pattern of living. In towns, and especially in great cities, family ties are usually much weaker than in villages; and the family ceases to be an economic as well as a social unit, as it is among peasants in most parts of the world. Nor are the ties of neighbourhood nearly so strong among city-dwellers as in the country, though they are much stronger in slums and old working-class areas than on new housing estates or in middle-class suburbs. Moreover, though the skilled craftsman still learns a trade for life, he is much less likely than the old-time craftsman to practise it for life in one employment, or even in one branch of industry; and much craft work has been taken over by a host of dexterous machine-minders, women as well as men, who can shift fairly easily from one branch of mechanised production to another, and therefore strike no deep roots in any one. Over and above all this, in great towns more and more people work in one place and reside in another, often at a considerable distance. This means not only much time spent in travelling, but also a much greater divorce between the human contacts of work and home. Wives do not know their husbands' work-mates or their wives. Husbands divide their social contacts between the work-place and the place of residence. The result is greater individual liberty in some respects — much less pressure of public opinion for conformity of behaviour within neighbourhood groups, much more latitude for men and women to develop their own separate social contacts, if they are so minded, and also much less domestic pressure upon adolescents and even on children still at school.

Our town-dwelling civilisation is a by-product of industrialism. Our towns have grown up round ports, upon coalfields, or wherever an industry has once taken root — for the presence of a few firms in a place, engaged in a particular type of production, has been a strong inducement to other firms to settle near by, in order to get the benefit of a common pool of suitable workers and the services of ancillary trades with which they need close relations. There were great cities before the Industrial Revolution; but they were few, and were mostly centres of government as well as of production or commerce. There were many small towns; but they were mostly rather market centres for the surrounding country than independent units in their own right. Those who lived in them were in close contact with the countryside: there was no clear line of division between the large village and the town.

Urbanisation, then, is the outstanding mark of modernity; and with it goes a transformation of the ways of living. The town-dwellers include a host of manual workers whose lives are passed in daily contact with machinery, and a lesser, but ever-growing, host of clerical and administrative workers in offices, public and private, banks and shops. Government, national and local, increases its demands on man-power at a prodigious rate; and there is a great growth of the professions, including many new ones which achieve recognition of their status in the professional hierarchy. Social stratification becomes much more complex: birth counts for less and education for more, and the educational system itself undergoes vast changes to adapt it to the conditions of a changing society.

In this modern capitalistic world the small economic unit survives in large numbers — small shops and offices, small firms engaged in building or manufacture, garages and a great many others. But more and more people are employed in large establishments, which are in many cases owned by concerns which operate many plants — for the scale of business organisation is often much larger than that of production. The individual employer is usually at the head of a small or at most a middle-sized business. The representatives of big business tend to be either financiers, with a finger in many pies, or managerial experts drawing large salaries — very often "self-made" men. They stand at the apex of large hierarchies of salaried administrators and experts, recruited from a wide variety of social groups, and without a great deal in common with the family-firm type of employer or with the small master or trader running a personal business. Technical progress, formerly to a considerable extent a matter of individual discoveries and improvements, often made by innovators without higher scientific or technological knowledge, comes to be more and more a matter of expensively organised research, which can be afforded only by the biggest firms or by collective institutions, private or public, or betwixt and between. Research laboratories employ a large body of trained lesser technicians, working under scientific leadership; and big productive firms also employ large numbers of technically trained experts. The proportion of employed persons engaged in actual productive operations in industry, after rising sharply during the earlier stages of industrialisation, tends to fall; the proportion of administrators, technicians, draughtsmen, clerks, computers and typists tends to rise. The proportion of transport workers first rises sharply and then becomes relatively stable. That of domestic workers in private houses first rises, and then falls off, but the number of those engaged in institutional services continues to increase sharply. Outside industry, such vocations as teaching, nursing and social work become more highly professionalised. The number of persons possessing some sort of professional qualification increases fast, particularly at the lower levels of remuneration. Recognised, collectively negotiated scales of remuneration spread from manual work to more and more professional and semi-professional occupations: Trade Unionism, ceasing to be mainly a monopoly of the skilled manual crafts, spreads upwards to the salaried grades as well as downwards to the less skilled workers. Businesses combine more and more, both to bargain collectively with employees and to regulate the market through trade associations and to represent economic interests in dealing with governments, which, turning their backs on *laissez-faire* notions, intervene more and more in economic affairs.

The town — with its aggregation of people dependent on wages, living mainly in rented dwellings, and without any family homestead to which they can return in time of trouble to share its poverty as recognised members of a group bound together by close traditional obligations — has to replace family solidarity by forms of collective provision, public or private, for meeting the calamities and insecurities of industrial civilisation. The forms taken by this development vary greatly from country to country. In nineteenth-century England, an intentionally inhumane and deterrent poor law existed side by side with a great expansion of voluntary charity—dispensaries, hospitals, relief agencies often animated by religious principles and with a strong preference for aiding only the " deserving " poor — or those who could make a plausible pretence of desert. Self-respecting workers and small traders built up, as means of escape from both poor-law stigma and the *de haut en bas* inquisitions of charity, their own agencies of mutual help — Friendly Societies, Penny Banks, Co-operative Societies and the like. During the age of *laissez-faire*, there was strong prejudice against the State entering into the business of " relief ", save as a last resort; and the poor law, conducted on this principle, earned the bitter hatred of the poor and impelled them to provide for their own needs as far as they could. But as the franchise became more democratic, and politicians had to bid one against another for poor men's — and later poor women's — votes, the pressure to develop public social services, free from the stigma of pauperism, increased. In Germany, Bismarck became the pioneer of State-organised compulsory insurance, which made the poor pay for the poor by equalising the burden; and other countries, before long, followed suit. But matters could not stop there: when it had been recognised that the State had an obligation to make collective provision for reducing the insecurities of life under industrialism, the politicians could not long stop short of providing a part of the money out of the proceeds of general taxation. In the twentieth century there was a very rapid extension of social services, spreading even to the United States, the final stronghold of *laissez-faire* notions, during the great depression of the 1930s. Dependence on public provision for meeting misfortune ceased to be regarded as a disgrace and became a normal thing for the entire working-class, and presently began to spread up the social scale to embrace the middle classes as well. Old Age Pensions, Children's Allowances, National Medical Services, free or highly subsidised higher education, subsidised housing, came in side by side with cash benefits in sickness, disablement and unemployment. In the economically advanced countries, social security became part of the programme of every political party aiming at a popular appeal.

In the nineteenth century, advanced economic systems existed only on a basis of private ownership and enterprise. There were public enterprises, national and local; but they were exceptional, and took their tone mainly from their capitalistic environment. It was commonly believed that capitalism, often called "free enterprise", was the only foundation on which economic productivity could be built. Throughout the century there were Socialists who attacked the prevailing system and called for public planning and control of production; but there was no actual economy based on public ownership. Not until the Russian Revolution of 1917 did a State go over to a comprehensive system of public enterprise; and there were many thereafter who contended that the new

States of the Soviet Union must speedily collapse because they were flouting both " human nature " and the " laws of political economy ". It was said confidently that no country in which the public owned industry would ever consent to set aside for capital development enough of its current productive resources to keep the industrial machine intact — much less to allow productivity to be improved. In fact, however, the Soviet Union has maintained over more than a quarter of a century the highest rate of capital investment ever known and, far from showing signs of economic breakdown, has leapt in a generation from gross economic backwardness to a position which allows it to challenge the most advanced nations. It may be said that this has been possible because the Soviet Union is not a consumer-controlled democracy but an authoritarian autocracy under Communist control; but, whatever the reason, the fact remains that capitalism has been shown to be not the *only* economic system capable of utilising modern scientific techniques and of undertaking great schemes of capital development. It remains to be seen whether Marx was correct in prophesying that capitalism, having served its purpose, would prove incapable of controlling the expanding powers of production and would in due course be everywhere superseded by some form of collective organisation of industry. To discuss that question is outside the scope of the present history; but the Soviet Union is by now an historical force and will have to be taken account of in its place. So will the evolution, in Great Britain and elsewhere, of " mixed systems " in which capitalism continues to exist side by side with a " socialised sector " and subject to a considerable element of public planning and control.

In the present study I shall go back no more than two centuries, though of course what happened in industry and agriculture, in transport and commerce, in the growth of towns and in the reshaping of class-structures after

1750 had its roots in a scientific revolution which began much earlier and was closely connected with the discovery of the New World and with the break-up of the medieval social order. I must take these and many other factors for granted, in order to keep my subject within manageable limits. The justification for starting at about 1750 is, not that there was a sharp break at about that point, but that, in the particular country which came to be the leader in the Industrial Revolution, it was in the second half of the eighteenth century that the pace of economic change was so speeded up as to involve sweeping changes in the ways of living of the people, in the pattern of town and country, and in men's thoughts about society.

The country in which this great change first came about was England — England rather than Great Britain as a whole, for only small areas in Wales and Scotland were much affected in the earlier stages. From England the Industrial Revolution spread out, to conquer other countries; but nowhere else, until much later, did it lead to quite so far-reaching an upset of the traditional ways of living. The story of the great transformation in its effective beginnings has to be told largely in terms of the English experience. Later, we shall see other countries joining in, each in its own rather different way. But it is pertinent to have in mind from the beginning that, after two centuries of unprecedentedly rapid economic change, the Industrial Revolution is still a long way short of having spread over the entire world. We have witnessed, in our own generation, its spread to Russia, where, under the Czars, it had barely touched the lives of most of the people. Even now it has spread only a little distance in India and in China, and hardly at all in a large part of Africa. Much of Latin America is still little touched by it, though there development has been rapid in recent years. A high proportion of the world's inhabitants are still living at standards which owe nothing to the enormous advances in productivity achieved by the use of modern techniques, and are still getting their livings by primitive methods which have changed but little for centuries past. Only now are men beginning seriously to ask themselves how and how fast the mastery of scientific and technological forces can be extended to the whole human race. Almost until now it has been usually taken for granted that there is nothing wrong in some nations enriching themselves while others remain sunk in primary poverty.

It is an unquestionable fact that the development of the social conscience in this respect among the citizens of the more advanced countries is due more to the emergence of the Soviet Union as a great industrial power than to anything else. If the Soviet Union has been able, in a single generation, to become one of the two most powerful countries in the world and to master the most advanced productive techniques, what should prevent other backward countries from following the same road? No doubt the Soviet Union, despite its prodigious advances, is still a poor country in terms of the average standard of life; but it has clearly started out on a road which will lead it before long, unless it is wrecked in war, to standards of living comparable with those of other developed countries. If Russia, why not China? Why not India? Why not every country, in proportion to its population and resources? Two centuries have spread industrialism over less than half the world. How long will it take to conquer the rest?

To this question I shall have to come back. It should be easier to estimate the prospects when we have seen how the Industrial Revolution has actually spread from country to country since its effective beginnings in England two centuries ago. Let us begin by trying to see what are the essential characteristics of this industrial system as it exists to-day, and then let us compare it with the economic society that existed in England about the middle of the eighteenth century, before the advent of power-driven machinery and factory employment had much affected the ways of living of the English people.

II

The Nature of Modern Industrial Society

THE economic system under which the more developed parts of the world are living to-day is one of predominantly large-scale production aided by very complicated and costly machinery and by the intensive use of power. Small-scale production continues to exist even in the most advanced countries; and the size of the majority of productive establishments is still fairly small, even in such countries. But large-scale production holds a key position in the total economy; and in many cases the scale of business organisation is very much larger than that of the factory or other productive unit. Land, water and air transport are also for the most part under the control of large organisations: the merchanting and distribution of goods show a more complicated pattern, varying greatly from place to place as well as from product to product. Agriculture, too, has nowadays its examples of large-scale production, though in most countries the typical productive unit is still relatively small: agricultural marketing tends more and more to large-scale unification among both sellers and buyers. Banking and credit are everywhere either conducted by large-scale agencies, or co-ordinated under large-scale control. The social services, as well as such public utilities as the supply of water, gas and electricity, have come to be more and more assimilated to the forms of large-scale business organisation — for example, public health services, and even education.

These methods of production, distribution and exchange — to use the traditional phrase — involve the aggregation into large masses not only of capital but also of labour in its highly diversified forms. They involve large-scale planning of the processes of investment and of scientific and technical research, not necessarily for whole countries, but at least on a scale corresponding to that of the business organisation itself. They involve extremely complicated structures of human beings and problems of human relations. They have led to an immense growth of towns and industrial areas and to a drastic change in the pattern of living, including vast migrations of persons both within countries and across national and continental frontiers. They have required, in order to feed and to supply with raw materials the centres of industry and commerce, a great opening up of previously undeveloped and sparsely inhabited areas, and have established a pattern of highly complicated exchanges between industrial and agricultural countries and districts. Finally, they have called into being in all industrial countries Trade Unions which more and more reproduce the large-scale characteristics of the business organisations they confront, and in nearly all agricultural countries extensive Co-operative organisations of farmers or peasants, far exceeding in membership the consumers' Co-operatives of the industrial areas.

This description of the characteristic economic structure of the modern world has been deliberately given in terms which disregard the difference between private enterprise and socialisation. It applies equally to the Soviet Union and to the United States, despite the vast differences between their economic and social systems. It emphasises the technological foundations of the modern economic order, which are broadly the same in all advanced countries however different their politico-economic arrangements may be. Whether or not some form of socialism is in process of superseding capitalism as the method of controlling the forces of production, distribution and exchange, the sheer compulsion of the technological developments creates business structures of a largely similar sort. It could not make a great deal of difference to the actual work done by most of the persons employed by Imperial Chemical Industries if that giant business were nationalised: it has not made much difference to the actual work of miners or of railwaymen who, in Great Britain, now work for public boards instead of privately owned joint-stock companies. Their pay, their status, their feeling about their work may, or may not, be affected: the work itself, and to a great extent the methods of organising it, are bound to remain essentially the same.

Until well on in the present century, the predominant pattern of politico-economic as well as of technico-economic development was broadly the same in all the countries which passed through an industrial revolution. Their form of development was capitalistic, in the sense that the instruments of large-scale as well as of small-scale production were for the most part privately owned, and the accumulation of capital and its investment in means of production, distribution and exchange were done by private persons or by groups of private persons under the stimulus of the profit incentive. There were cases of public, and also of Co-operative enterprise; but they were exceptional. The characteristic business structures of the developing industrial system were the enlarged partnership and before long what we call the "joint-stock company", the Americans the "corporation", and the French, more graphically, the *société anonyme*. These devices have made it possible to concentrate the control of capital resources in bigger and bigger concerns under unified direction, without the concentration of ownership in correspondingly few hands. They have also, to an increasing extent, transferred the function of saving for investment from the individual recipient of income to the directors of this massed capital, who can hold back from distribution to the shareholders such part of the profit as they think it wise to retain in the business in order to provide for its expansion. In effect to-day the shareholders do not own the businesses in which their money is invested: they own only certain limited rights to receive incomes out of the profits. The company, the corporation, the *société anonyme*, in effect owns itself: the shareholders have, as a rule, virtually no control over its doings: its real controllers are its directors, who are in practice self-co-opting, though they are formally elected by the shareholders' meeting, which few trouble to attend. These collective persons, recognised by the law of the capitalist countries as legal persons, are the controlling forces of the economic system. Often, one great company or corporation owns or controls many others: often, financial or banking corporations own or control many productive concerns. The shareholders, unless they belong to the directing *élite*, are passive, except at the moment when they make an investment in *new* shares. Many small and some middle-sized companies, and a few big ones, retain the character of family businesses; but in most of the big ones the controlling directors own but a small fraction of the total capital, and many of them are rather professional business organisers than capitalists in the older sense of the word.

When a business, or a whole industry, is nationalised, the board of directors, or the boards, give place to a public board whose members do not own any share in its capital. But the new board has to perform most of the same functions as the old ones, in respect of the actual conduct of the business. The main difference is that it becomes subject in some degree to control of high policy by the State — which may in practice mean much or little, according to the use which Ministers and Parliaments make of their power. The capital becomes State-owned; but, save where social revolution has brought with it confiscation of the rights of the previous owners, the nationalised business may still have to meet an interest charge for compensation, and, where it has not, the State usually levies a tax on the proceeds of the nationalised service. The employees continue to receive salaries or wages: the managers continue to manage and the supervisors to supervise. There may be changes in collective bargaining, more "joint consultation", even — as very recently in Yugoslavia — an element of "workers' control". But the sheer technical requirements compel the continuance of the same broad structure of work organisation, the same interconnection of jobs and routine arrangements, and — not least — much the same patterns of behaviour during the hours of employment. This does not mean that the differences are unimportant: it does mean that modern technology imposes a high degree of uniformity upon the actual conditions of men's working lives.

From the standpoint of those who work, the predominant environment thus comes to be one of membership of a large and complex productive group. The number of persons whose work is done either in isolation or in small groups remains large, even in the Soviet Union; but there is a constant tendency both for the proportion employed in large work-groups to increase and for many of the smaller groups to become less independent and self-contained. In particular, the growth of mass-production methods and of big establishments turning out repetition goods by highly standardised mechanical processes calls into existence a kind of producer who is required to develop, not a specialised skill, but a form of quickly learnable machine dexterity which is easily transferable from one operation to another. Highly skilled workers are needed to set up and to maintain the complicated machines; but the majority of those who operate them do not need to be more than, at most, semi-skilled. As against this, there has been a vast increase in clerical labour and in the numbers of technicians and administrators, and a fall in the proportion of employees engaged in actual productive operations. There has also been a sharp decrease in the proportion of unskilled heavy labour, much of which, in the large-scale industries, has been taken over by the machine.

The social correlative of large-scale industry is urbanisation. The proportion of urban to rural population differs greatly from country to country, even among the most advanced. Great Britain is the most urbanised of all the industrial countries, and has the lowest proportion of its people working on the land. The United States, with its vast area, retains a much higher proportion of land-workers and of country-dwellers, despite its intense development of industry and commercial operations. The Soviet Union is still more agricultural than industrial, but is increasing its industries and its urban population at a prodigious rate. But, widely as conditions differ from one industrially developed country to another, the tendency has been everywhere the same — towards a relative fall in the numbers of country-dwellers and land-workers, and towards more and more concentration in urban areas. The same tendency has appeared where modern industrial methods have been introduced into the less-developed countries. The mills of Calcutta and Madras and of Shanghai have produced problems of urban life closely akin to those which the Industrial Revolution in its early stages gave rise to in Lancashire and the West Riding.

This, then, is the type of society of which we are setting out to trace the broad stages of development over the past two hundred years. We can now proceed to see how different were the conditions and assumptions of economic life in England two centuries ago ; for, as we saw, England, as the first country to be radically transformed by the new forces, provides the natural starting-point for this study.

III

Two Hundred Years Ago

TWO centuries ago there were only a very few steam-engines, though the inventions of Savery and Newcomen were already half a century old. The Newcomen beam engines of 1750 had a very high consumption of fuel, and could be used only where there were plentiful supplies of coal near at hand. Moreover, the Newcomen engine was essentially a *pump*: its principal use was for raising water; no one had yet succeeded in devising a practicable method of using it to turn the wheels of machinery. The improvements of Watt and others, who succeeded in making engines both much more economical in their consumption of fuel and capable of imparting the rotatory motion which industry wanted, were still in the future, though very near. When power was used in industry, beyond the physical strength of men, it was the power of wind, or of water, or of horses set to tramp round and round in a circle turning a "gin" or "whim". Most industries still managed without any of these kinds of power. Most machines were turned by hand or by foot-treadle. The typical craftsman who used a machine tool turned it for himself, or sometimes had it turned for him by a helper — usually a boy. Many craftsmen made no use even of such machines, working entirely with hand tools.

Except in mining and in a few big waterworks, where pumping engines were coming more and more into use, the chief source of power was water — that of streams and rivers which either had a natural fall or could be dammed up to make one. Factories, where they existed, and workshops which needed power were nearly all located by running water; and sites which gave command of suitable water-power were much in demand. This limited urban concentration: the industrialist had to go to the water, and this meant placing most establishments away from the towns. It also gave an advantage to the hilly country of the north, which had many streams with a good natural fall. These streams mostly had the further advantage to the manufacturer of not being navigable; for on navigable rivers there was often sharp conflict between those who wished to use them for boats and barges transporting goods and those who proposed to dam them for the supply of power. Even after 1750, the earlier phases of the Industrial Revolution were based largely on the use of water-power. Richard Arkwright's most famous invention — the "water-frame" for cotton spinning — was so named for this reason. It was a spinning frame driven by water-power. In the great French Encyclopaedia there is a picture of a giant horse-gin used for driving textile machines. But horse-power was slow and inconvenient: water-power had great advantages, where it could be applied. Wind-power was too irregular to suit factory requirements, though it was of course extensively used for grinding corn, and also for land drainage.

Water-power involved a wide diffusion of the factories that employed it. You can still see the ruins of old textile mills as far afield as the Scottish Highlands. Robert Owen's famous factory at New Lanark, which had been founded by his father-in-law, David Dale, in partnership with Richard Arkwright, owed its location to the nearness of the Falls of Clyde: its original source of power was the river. Some factories using water-power were large; but most had to be small, because there was only a little water to serve them. The hills round Sheffield were studded with small establishments which used the small, swift streams to drive great hammers used in battering metal to remove impurities or to beat it into the required shapes.

Water was also the chief means of transport — the only means of moving bulky goods over considerable distances. England was a land of many small ports used for coastwise trade, as well as of a few large ones for ocean shipping. Industries producing heavy goods had to be near the sea or navigable water; and, as there were still no canals — unless one counts new river cuts through flat country — the rivers were all-important. River-improvements had been proceeding fast during the first half of the eighteenth century: dredging out channels, cutting off avoidable bends, struggling to get dams created for industry removed or by-passed, were all parts of the process. River navigation remained slow, circuitous, and in many cases much affected by seasonal shortage of water as well as by obstructive dams and bridges; but it was the only means of bulk transport between the interior and the sea coast. In a few districts it was possible for waggon-ways to bring coal and other bulky materials down from hilly country to the coast without mechanical power, but often with the aid of horse-power or of winches for getting over awkward places. But this was never practicable over long distances, or in more than a few areas, such as South Wales. Road transport had to be used, till true canals with locks began to be constructed in the latter half of the century, for carting bulky goods to the nearest navigable water; but it was both costly and made very difficult by the state of the roads, especially in winter. Lighter goods could be carried by land over longer distances in waggons, where the roads were good enough, or on horseback, in panniers along unmetalled tracks or narrow, stone causeways.

The main roads were considerably improved during

the first half of the eighteenth century, especially in southern England. It was an easy journey from London to Bath or Bristol, and the coaches already gave good service. But there was much less travel between the North and the South, and the roads from London to Lancashire, Yorkshire, the North-East and Scotland had still to be brought into a tolerable state. The main roads in the North, and the lesser roads everywhere, were still in a very bad condition. The great road improvers, such as Telford and MacAdam, were not yet born. The great coaching age was still far in the future. Folk travelled, despite the inconveniences — the richer on horseback or in post-chaises or private coaches, the middling by stage-coach, the poor by the huge stage-waggons, used mainly for transporting the lighter goods, or afoot. The mails, except on a few main routes, still went with post-boys on horseback: the national system of mail coaches did not begin until the 1780s.

The towns, except London, were all small, by modern standards. Nobody knows at all exactly what their populations were, either within their municipal limits, which were in most cases narrow, or including their suburbs and "ribbon developments" along the streams. Bristol, the biggest city outside London, is said to have had about 43,000 inhabitants in 1750, and Norwich about 36,000; Liverpool had about 22,000; Manchester and Salford, with their environs, may have had about 20,000, and Birmingham, with its environs, about the same number. Newcastle-on-Tyne, with Gateshead, probably had rather more; Hull was well under 20,000; Leeds and Sheffield well under 15,000; Nottingham about 11,000. London can be put at any figure from half to three-quarters of a million, according to the area included. It was the one really big urban centre; and the provisioning of it was a major problem, continually straining the inadequate transport facilities. London's coal and many of its other supplies, for export as well as for consumption, came by sea: the beasts for slaughter in the main walked in from the countryside, to be fattened up in the pastures of Essex and Hertfordshire before they were killed. Much of the country round London was given up to market gardens and dairy farms for the supply of the metropolitan market; and the port of London was the main point of entry for imports from Europe and from the East. West Indian and American supplies — tobacco, sugar and hardwood — came in largely through Bristol. Liverpool was developing fast as a port, but had not yet replaced Bristol as the main centre of the American trade, or become the main intermediary in the traffic between America and Western Europe.

The woollen industry was still, in 1750, by far the most substantial employer of industrial labour. It also linked together the interests of the landowning and the commercial classes. Using almost exclusively home-produced wool, it was Britain's foremost exporting industry, as well as first in the home market. The cotton industry was still a pygmy beside it, of less importance than the linen industry, though already growing fast.

There were in England three main centres where woollen goods were made — the Eastern Counties, the South-Western Counties and Yorkshire. These were all old-established centres; but, by 1750, Yorkshire was advancing at much the greatest rate and the Eastern Counties were relatively falling back, though Norwich remained a great producer of high-class worsted fabrics. Wool was largely grown in all these areas, and also in others which did not manufacture on a considerable scale. The weaver's trade counted as skilled, but not, except for pattern-weaving or for the finest products, as highly skilled. It could be learnt fairly easily, even without formal apprenticeship. It was a men's trade, carried on mainly in towns or in considerable industrial villages, with handlooms set up either in the weavers' cottages or in workshops attached to a small master's house — attic workshops being common in Norwich and other centres. Spinning, on the other hand, counted as an unskilled occupation, and was in the hands of women, aided by their children, as a domestic occupation which helped to eke out the scanty means of the family. The husband might be a weaver, a worker in some other industry, or an agricultural worker; for spinning was much more widely diffused than weaving in both towns and villages. It took several spinners to keep a weaver supplied; and, as demand increased, it grew difficult to find enough to meet the need. Hence the many attempts before as well as after 1750 to devise spinning machines that would speed up production; but none of these achieved success till after the middle of the century, and then for cotton well before wool — for cotton lent itself more easily to mechanical treatment. Just before the middle of the century Kay's invention of the flying shuttle had aggravated the problem by speeding up the weaving process; but it took a considerable time for Kay's device to come into general use.

The economic structure of the woollen industry varied greatly from district to district. Everywhere, the merchant was of great importance, dominating the market and passing back his orders to the producers. It can almost be said that the merchants were the only considerable capitalists in the industry, for actual production was hardly ever on a large scale. The merchants employed substantial numbers in scouring and sorting raw wool, in fulling, and in certain finishing processes; but they did not, save quite exceptionally, carry on the main processes of manufacture in establishments of their own. In the West Country, however, they were virtually the employers of most of the spinners and weavers. Commonly, they bought the wool raw and gave it out to be spun by cottagers for a piecework price, received it back and gave it out to be woven, and then perhaps gave it out again to be bleached or dyed. The men and women who worked for them on these terms were not legally in their employment: they received a payment for services rendered, rather than a regular wage. But they were, to all intents and purposes, employees, most of all where the merchants owned and hired out the looms on which the weavers worked. In some cases, however, the weaver who made his bargain with the merchant was himself a small master, employing hired labour as well as members of his family. He was then rather in the position of a sub-contractor.

In Yorkshire, the predominant system was different. There, for the most part, the weaving was done by small masters who owned their own looms, owned or rented their own workshops, and either employed cottagers to spin for them or bought their wool ready spun. These men carried through under their control the whole process of manufacture and sold their finished products to the merchants at the Cloth Halls of Halifax, Leeds, and other centres. Quite often, especially round Halifax, they combined farming with industry. They made much use of the hill streams, not mainly for power, except in fulling, but for washing, bleaching and dyeing. Socially, these practices produced a class structure very different from that of the Western Counties, with many small masters and independent workers, and much less power in the merchants' hands. The Norfolk weavers cherished a somewhat similar independence; but there the independent worker rather than the small master predominated, and the weaver was more a specialist craftsman performing a single process than a small-scale entrepreneur.

This situation was soon to be transformed by the development of factory production and by the use of power. In this the Yorkshiremen, already used to act as entrepreneurs and well provided with supplies of water-power (and later coal), showed themselves much more adaptable than the men of the East and the South-West. Yorkshire became the principal centre of the woollen and worsted trades, far outdistancing its rivals. This, however, was not till much later: in 1750 the rapid advance of Yorkshire was being achieved not by mechanisation but by cheaper and more efficient production and by an increasing concentration on cloths which the other districts denounced as low-grade imitations of their superior products.

The woollen industry has been described at length because it so dominated the eighteenth-century industrial scene. Other industries can be no more than summarily described. Silk had its highly mechanised factory at Derby, using secret processes for the making of the thread. London and, for ribbons, Coventry were the old weaving centres: Macclesfield and Leek were rising in importance. The linen industry was widespread, with its main centres in Scotland and Northern Ireland. The cotton industry, still largely producing mixed fabrics of cotton and linen or of cotton and wool, was beginning to develop fast in Lancashire and Cheshire. Framework knitting had its principal centres in the East Midlands — in and around Nottingham, Derby and Leicester. All these industries, in varying forms, reproduced the same essential structure of production carried on mainly in small workshops or in the workers' homes, with the merchants as the principal capitalists and the producers either virtually employees of the merchants or a mixture of small masters and wage-workers in their service. Because of the high cost of knitting-frames, frame-renting was especially common in the hosiery trades.

Next to textiles, the metal industries were the most important. In the iron trades, coal was in general use for smiths' work and was widely used in the preliminary processes of iron production. The Darbys at Coalbrookdale had already succeeded in making refined iron entirely with coal; but the knowledge of their methods was only beginning to spread to other areas. Steel was still a very expensive commodity, produced only on a small scale, and limited to use for cutting tools and a very few other purposes. Huntsman was at work on his new process for making cast steel, which he perfected about the middle of the eighteenth century; but this too was costly, though the process yielded a superior product. The iron industries were beginning their migration from the neighbourhood of woodland to that of coal: meanwhile, shortage of wood for fuel was causing considerable dependence on imported bar iron from the Baltic and from America. Of other metal industries, the brass and copper trades were the most important. Battery works, for pots and pans, were largely situated beside streams for water-power to drive the hammers: coppersmiths, brassfounders and finishers, tinsmiths and pewterers were all important skilled crafts. Coal-mining was increasing fast, as a supplier both of the metal industries and of the domestic hearth. But it was not highly organised, except in the North-East, which supplied the London market — by water — as well as local needs.

Leather, too, was a leading industry — for saddlery and upholstery as well as for boots and other clothing. Tanneries were among the bigger types of factory: the bootmaker, the saddler, and other leather-workers were skilled craftsmen to be found in every town and considerable centre of population. Breweries were another example of large-scale production. Printing and papermaking were hand industries, using no power: the latter, needing large supplies of pure water, was located beside streams, often away from towns. Printing, on the other hand, was essentially a town industry, with the hand compositor as its aristocrat among craftsmen.

Shopkeeping and innkeeping were the largest occupations outside productive industry. Outside the cities, shops were mainly concentrated in the market towns, which served the villages on market days with stalls as well as shops. Pedlars and hawkers were also numerous, touring the farms and villages on horseback or afoot. Shops were mostly small — the day of the big emporium was still a long way ahead — and many shopkeepers were also craftsmen, making or blending their own wares. The master-craftsman's workshop was often a retail outlet as well. In the provinces, the towns near many gentlemen's seats already had high-class shops, to serve the well-to-do, as well as shops serving the middle classes and the farmers. The poor bought largely at market stalls, or from hawkers, except in the biggest towns.

Inns and ale-houses, and also gin-shops, were very numerous. The posting inns on the main roads had not yet risen to the full glories of the coaching age; but they were rising. On market days, farmers gathered at the "ordinaries" in the market towns, and lesser inns and ale-houses were thronged with customers. In the villages, the innkeepers were often farmers as well. In the towns and on the main roads they had close connections with the coaching trade; and special legislation was needed to prevent them from acquiring undue influence on the turnpike trusts.

There are no figures to show the occupational, or the class, distribution of the population in the middle of the eighteenth century — none between Gregory King's estimate near the end of the seventeenth century and Patrick Colquhoun's near the beginning of the nineteenth. The position in 1750 was certainly much nearer to King's estimate than to Colquhoun's, but since King's day there had been a big increase in the number of skilled craftsmen and other industrial workers. King counted in his figures whole families, assigning dependants to the occupational group of the household's head. Here is a greatly summarised version of his estimate, beginning at the bottom of the social scale.

GREGORY KING'S ESTIMATE OF THE POPULATION OF ENGLAND IN 1688

(Each Group includes Dependants)

		Thousands
1.	Cottagers, Paupers and Vagrants (300,000), including workers in domestic industries	1,300
2.	Labourers, including agricultural and industrial labourers and miners	1,275
3.	Soldiers, Sailors and Seamen	220
4.	Skilled Artisans	240
5.	Shopkeepers and Innkeepers	225
6.	Farmers	750
7.	Small Freeholders	660
8.	Larger Freeholders	280
9.	Lesser Merchants, Lesser Clergy, Lesser Civil Servants	118
10.	Upper Merchants, Clergy and Civil Servants, Army and Navy Officers	104
11.	Lawyers and other Professional Men	145
12.	Squires	30
13.	Nobles, Baronets and Knights	27
	Total	5,374

The most notable features of this list are, first, the small number of skilled artisans and, secondly, the absence of any class of " employers " or managerial persons. The larger employers presumably appear among the merchants, the smaller mainly among the shopkeepers and artisans. Miners are counted, not as skilled craftsmen, but as labourers. Most textile workers are presumably among the " cottagers ". Farmers renting land are not much less numerous than freeholders of all grades. Farmers and freeholders together (1,690,000) are more numerous than labourers, including miners and industrial as well as agricultural labourers. The "lower classes" — the first three groups — together number 2,795,000, or 52 per cent of the total. Artisans, shopkeepers and innkeepers — the non-agricultural "lower middle classes" — number 465,000, or 8·7 per cent. The rest of the "middle classes", again excluding the agricultural groups, number 367,000, or 6·8 per cent (Groups 9-11). The nobility and squirearchy together number only 57,000 — just over 1 per cent. Finally, freeholders and farmers account for 31½ per cent out of the total.

These proportions show how rural a society England was at the end of the seventeenth century. Half a century later, the situation had not changed radically. Farming, on owned or rented land, was still by far the most numerous occupation; and besides the freeholders and farmers a high proportion of the labourers and cottagers also worked on the land. Enclosures of land (open fields and pastures as well as commons and waste) had been frequent from the beginning of the century, though not so numerous as they were to become during the Napoleonic wars. They had not, however, led by 1750 to really large evictions of cottagers, or to the pauperisation of the labourers. The mid-eighteenth-century labourers and cottagers were poor enough, and for the most part wretchedly housed; but they fed and lived better than the peasants and cottagers of France. Nor did they suffer, as the French and the Irish did, from absentee landlords who merely levied toll on their villages, without giving anything back. The majority of English squires lived in the country, and so did the nobility, at any rate for a part of the year. The resident landlords had in many cases a sense of responsibility for their tenants, and exercised it in a patriarchal way, dealing out a rough justice which exacted high respect for one's betters, but also often giving succour in time of need. In the village, where there was a resident squire, the church often became an appendage to the manor house, rather than a centre of spiritual things; and the parson was often a farmer as well, and not seldom a magistrate as colleague of the squire. But many rural parishes had absentee incumbents and were served by very ill-paid curates who were not admitted to "society". Curate, or parson, often took a share in the work of the village school, where there was one. There had been many Charity Schools started by the gentry during the earlier part of the eighteenth century, but by 1750 the movement had slackened off. Some villages had neither squire nor parson nor school, nor even sometimes a church. These were places where ownership of the land was diffused, and they were often the raggedest and least comely, with no one taking responsibility for their collective affairs. Some villages were entirely agricultural: in others the man's earnings from the land were eked out by the shilling or two his wife and children could get from spinning or lace-making or straw-plaiting or some other domestic industry.

Such was the England of two hundred years ago — a country of perhaps 6 million inhabitants ($7\frac{1}{4}$ for Great Britain as a whole); still mainly agricultural, though active in overseas commerce and a large producer of woollen goods for the world market; with no big towns outside London; ruled over by an aristocracy of noblemen and country gentlemen whose ranks were being reinforced by wealthy merchants who bought land and whose sons and daughters quite often made aristocratic marriages. In its upper ranges a cultured society, in which verse-making was a common accomplishment and the rules of taste were well understood — or believed to be — and the country gentlemen prided themselves on their agricultural prowess as well as on their classical taste. In its middle ranges, go ahead in economic matters, and increasingly individualistic in outlook and behaviour.

In its poorer classes, accepting in the countryside the rule and the patronage of the gentry, but in the industrial areas given to occasional riots in times of scarcity and high prices, and beginning to establish trade clubs of skilled workers, especially in the corporate towns. In matters of religion, England was a divided country. The aristocracy, except for a few Catholics, belonged to the Church of England, which was unenthusiastic, loyal to the State, and even largely Erastian. The rising middle classes were divided between the Church and the varying brands of Dissent—the older Dissent which looked back to the seventeenth century and was quite unlike the Wesleyan Methodism which was soon to spread rapidly among the middle and lower classes. In 1750 Dissent was strong among the skilled artisans, but not among the labourers, who, except in a few areas such as Norfolk and the South-West (and of course Wales), were either Church or nothing.

Except for the wealthier classes, who travelled extensively, this eighteenth-century England was a land of relatively little movement from place to place, and of human relations mainly among small groups. But we must beware of exaggerating its primitiveness. In comparison with a large part of the world to-day, it already possessed a highly developed economic system; and it was also remarkably advanced in comparison with the England of a hundred years before. England was not yet the world's leading country in economic matters, but it was well on the way to becoming so and to outstripping its great rival, France. France, before the Revolution, had greater factories than any in England; but they lived under royal patronage and produced luxury goods or munitions of war. In English economic history, the eighteenth century was the great age of the merchants and of small masters laying the foundations for the later emergence of the industrial capitalist class.

Most of all must we beware of thinking of eighteenth-century England as pre-capitalist, because it did not possess a considerable class of big industrial capitalists. Its economic system was already essentially capitalist, and had been so for a considerable time. But its capitalist leaders were merchants predominantly, and industrialists only in a secondary sense.

Eighteenth-century England was " capitalist ", in the first place, in that its economic structure required the accumulation of capital into substantial masses over a quite wide field and in that it had a considerable, prosperous and rapidly growing body of rich men who made their money by financing trade and production. It was capitalist, secondly, in that most of its manual work was done, not by independent producers making and selling their own products, but by wage-earners labouring — though often in their own homes — for an employer to whom the product — and often the instruments and materials also — belonged. And it was capitalist, finally, in the sense that all the essential institutions of capitalism — rich merchants, joint-stock concerns, banks and credit agencies, and even trade unions — were already in existence and playing an active part in its operation.

Yet this capitalism of two centuries ago was in many ways very unlike the capitalism of to-day, for it was essentially commercial rather than industrial. It was based for the most part not on the direct employment of large numbers of workers in factories but on the large-scale control by merchants of the buying and selling of goods made under conditions of small-scale production. The typical capitalist of the eighteenth century was a commercial man and above all a merchant engaged in foreign trade. The great joint-stock concerns of the time were in the main not industrial enterprises but trading ventures, such as the East India Company. The way to get rich was not primarily by making things but by buying them from those who made them and re-selling them at a profit. Merchant capitalism came into being before industrial capitalism, which became the dominant system only with the advent of the machine age.

There were of course some large factories even in the days before steam power. This was especially true in France, for in France large-scale manufacture was encouraged and subsidised by the State, and the granting of royal monopolies fostered the growth of large establishments. The Stuart kings had attempted to some extent to follow the same policy in seventeenth-century England, but after the Revolution of 1688 English industry developed with little or no regulation by the State, which confined itself to the control of overseas trade. Gild control in the towns had been relaxed and in many industries had almost disappeared, and the rise of new trades and the spread of industry over the countryside had completed the destruction of the old system of regulation that had come down from the Middle Ages. Except in the royal manufactures of France and in a small number of big establishments in other countries, small-scale production was everywhere the ruling practice of the time, and there was very little economic inducement in most trades to build big factories, for until the coming of power-driven machinery there was usually no economic advantage in manufacturing on a large scale. The only exceptions were found in a few industries where complicated machines driven by water-power were already in use, and to a small extent in mining. Thus there were, in both England and France, already large-scale mining enterprises, and isolated instances of large-scale production were found in both the metal and the textile trades. But it generally suited the capitalist best, instead of becoming a large-scale employer of labour, either to buy goods from small independent masters and confine himself to dealing in these goods, or to purchase the raw materials and put them out to workers to make up for him under the so-called " domestic system " of handicraft.

Under these conditions the independence of the master-craftsman was often more apparent than real, and he was, in many trades, much nearer to being a sub-contractor working for a particular merchant than to maintaining his status as an independent producer. Indeed, in the trades where the " domestic system " was fully in force, the independence of the actual producers was even less than this and they were in effect wage-earners working for capitalists who were only in name not their employers.

Nevertheless, the capitalist, since he did not, as a rule, assume direct control over the processes of production — save in certain of the finishing trades — remained more a merchant than an industrialist in his attitude and economic status. The system had, moreover, the effect, in the trades where it was in force, of preventing the accumulation of wealth in the hands of the master-craftsman and of preserving the monopolistic power of the merchants. This stood in the way of an extension of the scale of production, for the master-craftsman had usually no means of getting control of capital for the enlargement of his business, and the merchant preferred dealing with a number of small producers to becoming himself a large-scale employer. The new machinery, when it came, afforded in one trade after another the opportunity for the small man to rise, for the merchants themselves seldom made any attempt to turn themselves into industrial employers of a new kind. Only in mining, in certain branches of the metal trades, and in a few other cases where the methods of production were too expensive to be carried on without a considerable application of capital, had industrial capitalism struck deep roots before the advent of power-driven machinery.

In this economic system of two centuries ago, the textile industries occupied a position of unquestioned pre-eminence. The manufactures of woollen goods, of silks, and of linens were the leading industries and accounted for the largest volume of international trade. Next to them came the trade in imported luxuries, chiefly from the Far East, and the growing trade of Europe with the European settlements in the West Indies and on the American continent. The Dutch, the most flourishing mercantile people of the seventeenth century, had, by the eighteenth, lost their position of leadership, although they still retained a great carrying trade, especially up and down the coasts of Western Europe. France and England had come to be the great rivals in world trade both with the East and with the New World colonies of the West, and their rivalry dominated the economic situation through most of the century. In 1750, France was certainly in advance of England as an industrial country and well abreast of her in commerce, but the French, with their long land frontier and their military ambitions, their autocratic political institutions, and their attempt to regiment industry under strict national control, fell behind as the century advanced. Their overseas commercial ventures received no such sustained support from the Government as those of Great Britain, and their industries were weighed down by heavy taxes as well as by arbitrary restrictions. War cost them their imperial position in both India and America, and in both cases Great Britain fell heir to their domination. French industry, even so, remained, until the machine age, ahead of British in skill of workmanship and in its use of machinery based on water-power ; but French commerce fell more and more behind, and commerce rather than industry held in the eighteenth century the keys to economic growth.

Indeed, the very rapid expansion of British economic life as the century advanced was clearly based on commercial development rather than on progress in the arts of production. Invention in industry, though we are apt to think of it as the main cause of British economic growth, came rather as a response to widening commercial opportunities than as the original stimulus to the extension of trade; but of course it soon reacted powerfully on commercial development. The rapid growth of British prosperity depended mainly not on improved methods of production but on the successful expansion of markets abroad, which gave the merchant not only the means of disposing of a gradually increased quantity of British goods but also a position of pre-eminence in the entrepôt trade with Europe in both Asiatic and American products. British industry was doubtless quick to respond to these expanding opportunities, but the original impetus came much more from commerce than from industry itself.

Moreover, the first effect of commercial expansion upon industry was seen less in changes in the methods or scale of production than in a rapid growth upon the old lines. The woollen manufacture spread further and further over the country districts. It expanded in its old centres, the Western Counties and East Anglia, and it grew by leaps and bounds in its newer home in the West Riding of Yorkshire. The reasons for this growth are interesting. As we saw, the woollen industry of Yorkshire was, in the early part of the eighteenth century, far less capitalistic — far less dominated by the rich merchant clothier — than that of the Western or the Eastern Counties. The small master-manufacturers of Yorkshire showed themselves much more adaptable to the changing demands of the world market, especially for cheaper varieties of cloth, than the capitalist clothiers and their "domestic" workers, just as in the nineteenth century they were far prompter than their rivals in the introduction of the new machines. Yorkshire therefore steadily captured trade from the older centres of manufacture; but the total expansion of the woollen industry was so great as to leave room for all, and the merchant clothier showed no sign of being driven from the field until after the Industrial Revolution.

It would be difficult to over-estimate the importance to Great Britain of the growth of the American market during the eighteenth century. By 1750 North America was easily the leading market for British goods and above all for woollens, for iron and its manufactures, and for a wide range of other consumers' wares. Europe took indeed a far larger total of British exports than America, but this total included a high proportion of re-exports from America and from the Far East. Under the old "colonial system" Great Britain sought to reserve for itself a monopoly of the American market and to prevent the growth on the American continent of industries likely to compete with its own; and deep fears were entertained, when the American Colonies were lost in the War of Independence, that Britain's export trade would perish with its political authority. But in fact, when the war was over, British exports to America, far from falling, continued rapidly to increase. The source of British economic intercourse with the American continent lay not in Great Britain's monopoly under the colonial system, but in the real need of the Americans to exchange their agricultural produce for British manufactures. Protectionism in the United States did not begin its growth until after the end of the Napoleonic wars.

The eighteenth century was, then, above all a period of rapidly developing merchant capitalism, and its greatest material rewards went to that country which was in the best position for exploiting the possibilities of an expanding world market. Holland, in some respects admirably fitted for this rôle — for it had both a flourishing mercantile marine and an abundance of accumulated capital — lacked both the military power necessary for keeping its hold on the distant trade with Asia and America and sufficient manufacturing industries of its own to afford a secure basis for commercial expansion. France, despite its advantages in wealth, population, and manufacturing skill, both dissipated its energies over-much in the quest for military supremacy in Europe and kept its industry and commerce in too close tutelage for them to develop freely. Germany was still far too divided, and for the most part too backward in both industry and commerce, to make any bid for supremacy in distant markets. Upon Great Britain, therefore, the new wealth which arose from the opening up of trade with East and West was showered most abundantly, and the foundations of Great Britain's commercial supremacy were laid even before the great inventions had begun to revolutionise the methods of production. Indeed, the inventions were made and applied first in Great Britain mainly because British commerce had already opened up markets that were ready to absorb a greatly increased quantity of manufactured goods. Moreover, the British social system, economically if not politically, proved itself readily adaptable to the needs of the time, for in Great Britain the merchant class had already achieved social recognition and got the ear of Parliament. The British caste system was far less absolute than that of France, and the rich capitalist was able to buy land and to rise into the ranks of the gentry or even the nobility. His daughters married into the governing class and many of the members of that class were actively interested in commercial ventures. At the same time, the comparative immunity of British industry from State interference and gild regulation left it exceptionally free to adopt new methods as needs changed. The landed aristocracy continued to govern the country, but did so with a ready attention to commercial interests and with a minimum of bureaucratic interference. For, when the country gentlemen of England took the national government into their own hands and reduced the monarchy to a subordinate position, one use to which they put their power was to weaken the control of the centre over local administration, and one effect of this weakening was to free the internal development of industry from national control by the State. Puritan individualism, strong among the industrial and commercial classes, was thus enabled to take charge of economic development, and British industrialism did not have to do battle with the State for the right to live and to expand. The way was made smooth for the coming of the Machine Age ; and merchant capitalism blazed the trail for the Industrial Revolution.

IV

The Industrial Revolution

LET us move on seventy years or so and take our stand next fairly near the beginning of the nineteenth century, not long after the end of the Napoleonic wars. Both politically and economically world conditions had now become radically different. The Revolution in France had destroyed the *ancien régime* and Napoleon had swept his broom over Europe with effects none the less lasting because of his ultimate overthrow. The United States had become an independent country with a small but rapidly growing population and a no less swiftly developing economic system of its own. The countries of Western Europe, devastated by nearly a quarter of a century of warfare, needed time and opportunity to rebuild their shattered resources. Among them all only Flanders, about to become, as Belgium, an independent country, had advanced economically during the war, because it had been, under the French occupation, the effective centre of Continental industrialism, and its industries had been deliberately fostered during the period when British manufactures had been excluded from the Continental markets. France, worn out by warfare, had fallen definitely behind in the struggle for commercial supremacy. The French had lost their colonial empire and their manufacturers had had little chance of keeping up to date in the adoption of new productive methods. In Germany, though the seeds of national consciousness had been sown and the agrarian reforms of Stein and

Hardenberg had freed the serfs and prepared the way for the modernisation of Prussia, industrial techniques were still very backward, and internal Customs barriers were still far too numerous and oppressive to allow the successful commercial development of the country as a whole. Only Great Britain, immune from invasion and assured of maritime supremacy, had been in a position to exploit at all adequately either the new techniques of manufacture or the growing markets of the New World.

In Great Britain there had been no political revolution, and the reform movement, which had been gathering force before the wars, had been set back by the fears of Jacobinism which haunted the governing classes. Political agitation had been successfully repressed by Pitt and his successors; but economically there had been two distinct revolutions acting and reacting on each other — a revolution in agriculture and a revolution in industry. Of these two, the agrarian revolution, speeded up immensely by the war-time demand for the largest possible supply of foodstuffs, had been up to 1815 very much the more widespread and decisive in its effects. True, the cotton industry had risen with extraordinary swiftness from a position of quite minor importance and had become the leading industry of the country, and there had also been a great development in mining and in the metal trades. But even in 1815 the change in the British countryside was still very much more far-reaching than the change in the structure of industry or in the towns; for in the villages a whole population had found its ancient ways of living radically altered by the rise in prices and the pauperisation of the labourers under the Speenhamland system, as well as by the spread of enclosure and of scientific agriculture. Migration on a large scale from the countryside to the new industrial areas had set in despite the obstacles put in its way by the law of settlement and by the sheer difficulties of movement over long distances.

Agricultural changes had indeed been proceeding fast in Great Britain long before the Napoleonic wars. " Townshend's turnips ", Jethro Tull's " horse-hoeing husbandry " and Bakewell's improvements in stock-breeding all belong mainly to the period between 1750 and 1789. There was a constant movement for the enclosure of agricultural land all through the eighteenth century, and Arthur Young had made his famous tours of the English countryside well before the Revolution in France ; but the wars speeded up prodigiously the pace of agrarian change. They raised the prices of wheat, of meat, and of every kind of agricultural produce, and created an insatiable demand for an increased supply both to feed the growing population at home and the armies abroad and to make up for the devastation of a large part of the European continent and the cutting off of Continental supplies. The rapid rise in prices enriched landlords and farmers alike, while it impoverished the unfortunate labourers, whose wages, except in the Northern Counties, failed to keep pace with the swiftly advancing and wildly fluctuating cost of living. There was the strongest possible inducement both to bring waste lands under cultivation and to improve farming methods on lands already in use. But these things could not be done without breaking up the old village system ; and it was broken up, with remarkable effects in terms of total productivity but with a ruthless disregard of social consequences and of the hardships inflicted on the labouring class.

There is no room in this study for more than a glance at the social and economic consequences of this revolution in agrarian methods and in the life and work of the typical English village. The sufferings which it involved for the rural workers were accentuated both by the war, with its accompaniments of scarcity and high prices, and by a simultaneous shrinkage of opportunities for industrial employment in the rural areas, which was brought about by the development of the factory system and the decline of domestic by-employments. After delays caused by the difficulties of internal migration, the displaced villagers and their children provided the chief supply of labour for the new factories, and without this reservoir of dis-employed labour the revolution in industry would perforce have been greatly slowed down. Even as matters were, it was impeded in its earlier stages by a shortage of labour, and the delivery of pauper apprentices into factory bondage by the poor-law authorities of the larger towns was due directly to this shortage and ceased as soon as rural de-population had provided the industrial districts with a plentiful supply of "free" labour. The two revolutions in agriculture and in industry thus worked in together. The agrarian changes expelled the surplus population from the countryside and, after a transitional period of acute maladjustment with a surplus of labour in the south and a shortage in the new industrial areas, the Industrial Revolution absorbed the redundant country-men into the new mines and factories.

We must not, however, exaggerate the extent of the changes which had come about in British industry by 1815, for at that date there had been in the great majority of industries no radical change in the methods of production, though there had been a great increase in the quantity of goods produced. Only one industry, cotton spinning, had gone over completely, even in England, to machine production, and even in the cotton trade weaving was still done in the vast majority of cases on the handloom, the power-loom being still usable only for the simpler kinds of manufacture. The woollen industry was a long way behind cotton in introducing the new machines, and the lesser textile trades had hardly begun to use them at all. The output of coal and of iron had risen rapidly, and mines were deeper and iron-works larger and more capitalistic than in the previous century. The demand for war materials in England, as elsewhere, had given a stimulus to the metal trades; and this war demand had affected them much more than any change in industrial processes, for most, even of the new machines, were still made largely of wood, and the great demand for iron from the railways and from the engineering trades was still to come. The steam-engine, radically improved by Watt and adapted for turning the wheels of manufacturing machinery, was of course steadily making its way, and at such factories as Boulton & Watt's works at Soho, near Birmingham, the new skilled trades of mechanical engineering were being rapidly evolved. The old-fashioned millwright, a maker and repairer of wooden machinery, was being gradually replaced by the skilled fitter and turner and the other typical crafts of steam-engine-making. But these new trades were still in their infancy, and in most industries the application of steam-power had still hardly begun. Mines, waterworks and breweries still accounted for a large part of the total demand for steam-engines, and water-power was still the most important source of energy even for the growing factories in the textile trades. As late as 1839 over one-fifth of the horse-power in the cotton factories was still supplied by water-wheels, and in woollen factories over two-fifths. In the whole of Birmingham there were only 42 steam-engines in 1815, and only 120 even in 1830, but by 1840 this latter number had been doubled.

Even in England, then, the introduction of steam-power was slow and hesitant at first, and on the continent of Europe it was much slower still. Great Britain forbade the export of machinery and the emigration of skilled artisans up to 1824; and though both these prohibitions were largely evaded, there were serious obstacles in the way of the spread of mechanisation abroad. Even the English manufacturers had great difficulty in finding skilled labour and in devising suitable tools for the making of the new machines, and these obstacles were far more formidable in other countries. In France, William Wilkinson started the famous Creusot iron-works as early as 1780, and another Englishman, Milne, began making textile machinery there at about the same time. But except in mining, the steam-engine was introduced very slowly into French industry and the Creusot establishment was quite exceptional in its use of the most up-to-date methods.

In the economic world of 1815 there were no steam railways, though a few pioneering experiments had already been made in the application of steam-power to land transport on roads. There were only a very few steam vessels, for use on rivers and lakes, in Great Britain and America, and not for ocean voyages; and these were still only in the experimental stage. Machines, even in England, were still driven much more by water-power than by steam, and except in cotton spinning and certain branches of the metal trades the factory system was still in a rudimentary stage. What has been called the "Industrial Revolution" took place, even in Great Britain, much more after than before 1815. It came, in fact, when the wars were over and the immediate post-war crisis had passed.

The United States of America, while behind Great Britain, was well abreast of continental Europe in the introduction of steam-power. The first American steam-engine is said to have been erected at Philadelphia in 1773, and the Americans soon began to experiment with the use of steam-engines both for dredging and for river navigation. Flour-mills and breweries also began to use them at an early stage, and American industrialism, being a new growth, was often able to begin with steam-power without the need for a gradual transformation of its industries from the old basis to the new. The Americans became active as designers also, and the typical American steam-engine diverged at an early stage from the British standards, but its principal development in the United States took place after 1820.

Apart from the extraordinarily rapid rise of the cotton industry in Great Britain, the most notable differences between the economic world of 1815 and that of 1750 lay, not in the widespread use of mechanical power, but rather in the great advance of British overseas trade and in the very rapid growth of America both as a market and as a source of supply for Europe; in the definite worsting of France in the struggle with Great Britain for commercial and naval supremacy; in the opening-up of South America by the breakdown of the exclusive colonial system of Spain; in the rise of Belgium after the reopening of the Scheldt; and in the wholesale destruction of European feudalism by French armies and French example. Maritime power and immunity from invasion had at this stage done far more than steam to consolidate the mercantile supremacy of Great Britain.

Above all, the change from 1750 to the nineteenth century was a change in mental attitude. The old State systems of the earlier eighteenth century had seemed to most people essentially stable and permanent. Both French absolutism under Louis XIV and English aristocracy under the Revolution settlement had appeared to rest on the settled and secure adjustment of class relationships and political power. There were Jacobites in Great Britain, and in France there were reformers who held up the English Revolution of 1688 as a shining example; but England looked as unlikely to become an autocracy as France looked unlikely to base its government on a coalition between the aristocrats and the rich *bourgeoisie*. But after 1815, although Napoleon had been exiled and returned monarchs all over Europe were endeavouring to re-establish the *ancien régime*, although the English aristocracy had made short work of English Radicalism and the unreformed Parliament was still in power, although *liberté*, *égalité*, *fraternité* seemed everywhere to have suffered a moral as well as a political defeat, the old security of established institutions had irretrievably departed. The North American colonists had thrown off the authority of Great Britain, and South America was busily preparing to throw off that of Spain. Neither Bourbons nor German princes, though they were back on their thrones, could hope again to rule their dominions in the old way. Revolution was brewing in Spain, and not all the might of the Holy Alliance could stabilise the Peace Settlement of 1815. Free enterprise and nationalism were in the air, and men had to breathe the air of capitalism whether they liked it or not.

Great Britain was favourably placed for putting itself at the head of the new forces, not only because it had come out of the war rich and with territory intact and undevastated, but also because the English and the Scots found it easier than other European peoples to adapt their mental habits to the needs of the new time. The British aristocracy had never formed a closed system, and the rise of the merchant class in the eighteenth century had bridged the gulf between the old forces and the new. Pitt's distribution of honours and rewards, made in order to popularise the war and to ensure the supply of money for its conduct, had helped to dilute the aristocracy with new men who looked at the world with the eyes of commerce. Legitimism had little following in England, which believed in parliamentary monarchy under aristocratic control. Thus, when English commercial interests demanded the recognition of the revolting South American Republics, no appeal to the Divine Right of Kings was likely to stand in the way. British trade with North

America was also far too profitable for the British to go on thinking of the Americans as rebels who ought to be boycotted. In 1815 the new class of industrial employers was hardly ripe for political recognition, but as soon as it was ripe, in 1832, it won its share in political power with singularly little difficulty. By then, thanks to the enclosures and the high agricultural rents of the war years and to the profitable use of the new wealth which had come into the hands of the old governing class, the English aristocracy had become largely a plutocracy and the new rich had hardly to do more than show their credentials in order to gain admission to the political circle. Cotton spinners such as Peel, who were gentlemen as well, had prepared the way for cotton spinners who made no claim to be gentlemen. Dukes who owned coal-mines could not afford to turn up their noses at coal-owners who had the misfortune not to be dukes.

Thus the Great Britain of 1815 was already commercialised through and through, as the Northern States of America were commercialised, but as continental Europe, except Holland and Belgium, still was not. Great Britain had already destroyed its peasantry and made international commerce the foundation of its wealth and power. Its governing class, largely commercialised too, through the Peels, Huskisson, Canning and other young Tories as well as through the new Whigs, was alert to promote economic development, and was well aware, even before it was prepared to concede the reform of Parliament, that the country had to be governed in accordance with commercial interests. Great Britain had thus the mind, as well as the material equipment and the opportunity, to take the lead in world economic advance. British success in devising and applying the new mechanical forces was fully as much consequence as cause of the thorough-going commercial outlook of the middle and of a large section of the upper classes.

V

A Hundred Years Ago

LET us take our stand next at about the middle of the nineteenth century. We find ourselves in a world fully as different from that of 1815 as the world of 1815 was from that of a century before. During the first half of the nineteenth century the pace of economic change had been enormously speeded up and — the greatest revolution of all — the new power of steam had been successfully applied to the transport of men and goods by both land and sea as well as to production. This mechanisation of transport was indeed for most of the world still at an early stage, but by 1850 it had already produced an immense effect both on the scale of commerce and industry and on the structure of capitalist business. The coming of the railways had not only given the iron trade a new key position in the industrial system but had also revolutionised the nature of the processes of investment and prepared the way for the expansion of joint-stock ownership to large-scale enterprise as a whole. It had also greatly intensified the tendency towards exports of capital from the developed to the less-developed parts of the world.

In 1850 the evolution of the railways was far ahead of that of steamships. Although the *Savannah* had crossed the Atlantic as early as 1819, using steam-power as an auxiliary to her sails, and although by 1838 vessels using only steam-power had begun to make the Atlantic crossing, the great growth of steam shipping came only after the turn of the century, and up to 1850 the steamship was mainly of use for river navigation, for quite short sea voyages, and for the transport of passengers rather than of goods. The early steamships had such clumsy engines and needed to carry so much coal, in the days before fuel consumption had been reduced and coaling stations set up all over the world, that it was impracticable for them to transport heavy cargoes. The early ocean-going steamships were liners and not tramps, and America owed its pre-eminence in the building of steam vessels during the first half of the nineteenth century to the importance of its river and lake navigations — the only effective routes to the interior before the building of the railways.

Even as late as 1850, then, the steamship, with half a century of experiment behind it, had not been successfully applied to the carrying of heavy merchandise, and the great bulk of goods was still carried across the seas in sailing vessels. British pre-eminence in shipping and shipbuilding was still in the future. It came only with the rapid change from sail to steam and from timber to iron just after the middle of the century.

Railroad transport had advanced much further by 1850. The first public steam railway in Great Britain — the Stockton and Darlington — was opened in 1826, and there were already 6600 miles of line in operation in 1850 as against under 2000 in 1843. The United States opened the first section of the Baltimore and Ohio Railroad in 1830 and by 1850 had over 9000 miles of line at work. Ten years later the American total was over 30,000 miles. On the continent of Europe development was much less rapid. France had its first experimental line in 1830, but large-scale development did not begin until the 'forties, when it was largely financed by British capital and carried out with the aid of British engineers. In 1850 France had still only 2000 miles of railway and Germany only 3600, and in both countries almost the whole of the construction had been done since 1840. At the turn of the century the remoter countries still had hardly any railways at all. Russia possessed only 300 miles in all its vast area; Italy, 270 miles; Holland, 100; Denmark, 20; Switzerland, 16. Outside Europe and the United States railway-building had hardly begun. Canada had 70 miles in 1850, and India and Australia none at all until 1853.

Railway transport then, until after the middle of the century, was practically confined to Western Europe and the United States, but within these areas its effects had already been startling. In Great Britain, despite the development of canals, the transport problem had become steadily more acute as the Industrial Revolution advanced, and until the advent of the railways the growth of industry and commerce was seriously held up in the hilly areas of the North and in Wales, and also to a considerable extent in all the central part of the country. Birmingham and Sheffield and all the English Midlands owed their rapid economic development mainly to the railways; and the great British engineering industry, which became the chief supplier of capital goods to the less developed parts of the world, was built up at first much more on the demand for locomotives and railway material than on the growing use of machinery for productive operations.

In the United States the railroads played an even more dominant part in economic growth, for they were the indispensable means of opening up the vast regions lying to the west of the older settlements along the Atlantic and up the navigable rivers. The westward movement of population had indeed begun long before the first railway was built, but the settlers in the interior either clustered round the rivers and the great lakes or found themselves isolated from the outside world and with very restricted opportunities of producing for an outside market. Only with the extension of railway transport were the great grain-growing and stock-raising areas of the American continent opened up; and only the railways made possible the enormous increase in population during the latter half of the nineteenth century. These effects, however, made their appearance mainly after 1850, for at the turn of the century the large-scale export of wheat from America to Europe had hardly begun. In that year the United States exported in all 12 million bushels of wheat. By 1870 the quantity had risen to 60 million bushels, and by 1880 to nearly 300 million.

The first great difference, then, between the world of 1815 and that of 1850 lies in the extension of the use of steam-power from production to transport, but of course the older tendencies were also continuously gathering force. As we saw, except in cotton spinning, coal-mining, and a few branches of the metal trades, large-scale production had not advanced far in 1815, even in Great Britain; but between that date and the middle of the century the transformation went on apace. The power-loom, which had been invented by Edmund Cartwright towards the end of the eighteenth century, was at first too cumbrous for effective use, and only subsequent improvements made it a commercial proposition. It was introduced into the weaving of cotton goods very rapidly after 1815 and began a little later to invade the woollen industry as well. By 1850, in the major textile trades, handloom weaving had become of minor importance, though it still survived in the remoter districts and for certain special kinds of fine weaving. The jacquard loom — a French invention of the Napoleonic period — had, however, been harnessed to steam-power and was capable of weaving elaborate patterns.

This expansion of mechanised methods from the spinning to the weaving of cotton was accompanied by an enormous increase in output. British production of cotton cloth had grown tenfold between 1785 and 1820; and it grew again fivefold between 1820 and 1850. The other textile industries expanded much more slowly, and cottons had easily displaced woollens from their old position as the leading British export. But even of linen, despite the increased competition of the cheaper cotton goods, the output more than doubled in both Great Britain and Ireland during the first half of the nineteenth century.

Apart from the cotton trade, the greatest advance was in the metal industries. The production of pig-iron in Great Britain rose almost tenfold between 1810 and 1850 and more than threefold between 1830 and 1850, following the advent of the railway era. In the 1840s British pig-iron accounted for more than half the total world output, and the British production was more than four times as great as that of the United States, the second largest producer. The production of steel was everywhere still on a very small scale, for steel was still very expensive to produce and was used only for a very limited range of purposes, such as the making of tools. But in this case, too, Great Britain was by far the largest producer, with five-sevenths of the estimated total world output of 1850. Germany was the only other important producer of manufactured iron goods, with France a long way behind.

This rapid expansion of the metal trades centred mainly round the demand for railway material and round the growing use of steam-engines and machinery made of metal. Whereas the cotton trade, from the first, exported the greater part of its product, the iron industry in the first half of the century found its principal markets at home, though in the 1840s the foreign demand for both railway material and machinery was growing fast. Only when the work of building the British railways had been mainly done, and the home demand was ceasing to expand at a sufficient rate, did British ironmasters, engineers and railway and bridge contractors seriously set out in quest of foreign markets. In the case of railways this process had begun before 1850, but it did not assume outstanding importance until rather later. In 1850 the epoch of large-scale export of capital from Great Britain had hardly begun. What overseas lending there was was still mainly to Governments rather than either to foreign industrial borrowers or for the setting up of British-owned productive enterprises abroad.

In comparison with Great Britain, both France and Germany had made but modest economic advances during the first half of the nineteenth century. France stood next to Great Britain as a producer of cotton goods, but in 1850 the French output was less than one-third of the British. In the woollen manufacture, on the other hand, the British output barely exceeded the French, and in silk France was a long way ahead. In all three trades Germany was far behind France, and the introduction of machinery into the German textile manufactures proceeded very slowly indeed. The aggregate value of British foreign trade in 1850 was greater than that of French and German trade combined, and nearly three times as great as that of the United States.

Nevertheless, America had made tremendous advances in almost every field of productive activity. While the population of Great Britain doubled — from 10½ millions to 21 millions — during the first half of the century, that of the United States rose from 5·3 millions to over 23 millions. This increase was due much more to a rise in the number of births in the country than to immigration, which became much more considerable after the middle of the century. The United States in 1850 remained predominantly an agricultural country, but American manufactures were also growing fast and were finding their outlet in the rapidly expanding home market, without much need to seek customers abroad. In 1850 over two-thirds of the value of American exports was accounted for by raw and semi-finished materials and foodstuffs, and only one-eighth by fully manufactured goods. Raw cotton was the most considerable export, and Great Britain the principal market; but the expansion of foreign commerce was very slow in relation to the rise in the value of production. The United States was already well launched on a policy of Economic Nationalism behind a high tariff wall, and abundant natural resources made it easy to pursue such a policy without lowering standards of life to any noticeable extent, if at all.

American opinion, indeed, had turned at an early stage towards aprotectionist policy. The earliest American tariffs had been levied mainly for revenue, but the influx of European goods after the close of the Napoleonic wars led to a strong demand from the home manufacturers for protection, and from 1816 to 1833 the United States tariff moved steadily and rapidly upwards. The tendency was then for a while reversed, under pressure from the agrarian interests concerned largely with exports. Between 1833 and 1860 tariff revisions were on the whole in a downward direction. But import duties remained fairly high; and on the whole the American policy of relying chiefly on the development of home resources for home consumption was never in doubt. The United States imported foreign immigrants as it had imported negro slaves until 1808; but for the most part it produced and consumed both commodities and labour, free or slave, at home.

The Missouri compromise of 1820 had done something to limit the area over which slavery was to be recognised, and to save a large part of the rapidly developing West from the curse of slave labour; but in 1850 slavery had not yet been successfully confined to the South-Eastern States, for Nebraska and Kansas were admitted to the Union as Slave States as late as 1854. The settlement of the slave issue by civil war was still a decade ahead, and in the meantime the growth of the cultivation of cotton was preserving negro slavery as a live and growing institution in the South. In 1810 there had been one million slaves in the United States. There were over three millions in 1850, and over four millions when the Civil War broke out.

The other leading countries of the world were, at any rate, immune from the evil of slave labour. Great Britain abolished the slave trade in 1807 and slavery itself throughout the British Empire immediately after the Reform Act of 1832. Napoleon, during the Hundred Days, made a final end of French slave-holding, which had already been abolished by the Convention in 1794. In some other countries not only slavery but even the slave trade endured much longer. Slavery survived in the Dutch Indies until 1863 and in Brazil till 1871. Spain did not finally suppress the slave trade until 1865; and it remained in being inside Africa long after that. Indeed it was not wholly stamped out even in the twentieth century, for example in Abyssinia; but after the freeing of the West Indian negroes — with generous compensation to the planters — in 1833, the United States was left as the one great slave power.

Great Britain, however, though Parliament had put an end to negro slavery, was often denounced in the early nineteenth century for tolerating in the mines and factories at home conditions even worse in a material sense than those of the slaves on the West Indian plantations. Reformers of all schools of thought, from William Cobbett and Robert Owen to Edwin Chadwick and Lord Shaftesbury, depicted the working lives and the home conditions of the children and the women in the mines and the cotton factories in terms which impressed themselves on the imagination of their contemporaries and have continued powerfully to affect the judgment of economic historians. Again and again those who denounced negro slavery abroad but were blind to the sufferings of the operatives at home were castigated as hypocrites by the factory reformers. But there was something about open slavery which shocked the public conscience of the early nineteenth century even when it was inaccessible to even the most lurid accounts of conditions in the working-class areas of Great Britain. The basis of this feeling was largely religious; for slavery was felt to be inconsistent with the profession of human brotherhood under God and a denial of the divine institution of the family. But to this sentiment was added the deep belief of the influential leaders of economic opinion in the virtues of free contract. Slavery, it was alleged, not only produced evil material conditions and an inhumane and unchristian type of civilisation but also violated the principle of *laissez-faire* which contemporary opinion regarded as the essential driving force of material progress. Slavery, therefore, had to go, but it took much longer to bring about effective reform of working and living conditions in the spreading industrial towns.

Thanks to the reports left behind by the social reformers of the early nineteenth century, it is usual to paint a gloomy picture of the economic condition of the working-classes in England during the period which culminated in the "Hungry 'Forties" and to attribute mainly to the new industrialism the misery and squalor revealed by these contemporary documents. There is indeed no reason to doubt the absolute veracity of the devastating exposures contained in Edwin Chadwick's famous reports on the *Health of Towns* and the *Sanitary Condition of the Labouring Population*, or in such books as Friedrich Engels's *Condition of the Working Classes in England in 1844*, or the summing-up of the available evidence in Mr. and Mrs. Hammond's *Town Labourer* and their other books. Judged either by modern civilised standards or by the standards of what could have been done at the time had the new industrialism been directed with reasonable forethought and humanity, the situation of the workers in those days was miserable in the extreme; but it does not follow that the changes in industry and agriculture — for in this connection the two cannot be divorced — had made working-class conditions actually worse in a material sense for the workers as a whole than they had been during the preceding century. The more light we get on conditions of living among the poor before the Industrial Revolution, the nastier, on the whole, they appear. In the older towns there had been a festering mass of poverty, drunkenness and crime long before the coming of the Machine Age. The village labourer, even with rights of common and sometimes a patch of land of his own, lived wretchedly near to destitution and often in a state of almost servile dependence on the squirearchy; and the worker under the "domestic system", making goods in his home as a piece-worker for the merchant capitalist, was fully as much exposed to the hazards of unemployment as his successor the factory operative — and often even worse paid.

There were not, indeed, in the eighteenth century such excesses in the exploitation of child labour for incredibly long working hours as marked the earlier phases of the new industrialism, nor are there such dramatically pitiable stories to tell of the workings of the earlier system as have been told of the decline and fall of the handloom weavers and the dispossession of agricultural labourers and peasants by mass enclosures managed almost exclusively in the interests of the well-to-do. There cannot be any doubt that during and immediately after the Napoleonic wars intense misery was caused among the workers by the violent fluctuations in the cost of living and by the constant disturbances to the course of trade. But these extremities of suffering were probably due more to the war than to the revolution in industry. The huge rise in prices during the war left wages lagging behind and had caused the enclosure movement to be pressed on ruthlessly because of the high profits which could be derived from wheat-growing under the exceptional conditions of war-time demand; and when the war was over the difficulties of agricultural adjustment and the uncertainties of the world market and of monetary conditions caused intense dislocations which persisted for a long time.

On the other hand, as the Industrial Revolution gathered force in Great Britain, some part of the increasing wealth to which it gave rise went into the pockets of the skilled artisans, especially in trades which were not readily susceptible to mechanisation. The improvement in the wages and prospects of employment in these trades consequent on the brisk demand for their labour has to be set against the miseries of the handloom weavers and of the victims — mainly women and children — of the new factory system. On balance, it is not easy to say whether, up to the 1840s, the Industrial Revolution had made things better or worse in a purely material sense for the working class as a whole. The changes had reacted favourably on some sections and unfavourably on others; and, special cases apart, the adverse effects had been psychological rather than sheerly material. But by 1850, at least, it is safe to say that the working class as a whole was in a material sense substantially better off than it had been at any time in the preceding century.

The final indictment of the new industrialism is not that it actually reduced working-class standards of consumption, except in certain parts of the countryside and for certain groups of workers, such as the handloom weavers who fought a long losing battle with power-driven machinery. The charge is rather that it created in town and country alike a vast mass of human unhappiness and disorientation. The villages, with their land enclosed and the auxiliary earnings of domestic industry taken away, suffered from a surplus of landless workers who had lost their place in society. The teeming factory towns, with their insanitary dwellings and their utter lack of collective services, offered none of the means to happiness to the uprooted country-dwellers by whom they were largely peopled. The workers hated the harsh discipline of the factories and caused it to be harsher by rebelling against it; and the acute competition among employers and the extreme instability of markets led to sudden, sharp fluctuations in earnings and to alternations of overwork and unemployment which made provident housekeeping almost impossible. Despite the rapid advance of production, bankruptcies and closures of factories were common, and often spread disaster. Finally, employers, facing acute competition and eager to make high profits to add to their inadequate resources of capital, resisted ferociously every attempt of the workers to organise for the improvement of their conditions.

By the middle of the century, however, the growing-pains of the new system were mainly over. With the new abundance of capital which was being made available for economic development by the growth of the joint-stock system, employers had no longer the same reason for fighting bitterly against wage advances as they had when every penny spent in wages seemed to be so much subtracted from the supply of capital for the expansion of industry and the increase of future wealth.

Shortage of capital is indeed a characteristic feature of the development of modern industrialism in its earlier stages. It exists to-day, for example, in India, holding back the growth both of machine industry and of better agricultural methods, and putting powerful obstacles in the way of a higher standard of living for the Indian workers. Its effects have been mitigated — though not, as we shall see, without undesirable consequences — in the spread of industrialism from one country to another, by the growth of overseas investment, which has enabled the poorer countries to draw by borrowing on the developed productive capacity of the more advanced. But Great Britain, being first in the field, had to build up its new industries mainly out of its own resources, as Russia, for other reasons, has had to do in our own day. This was achieved partly by applying to the expansion of industry the profits of an already flourishing and expanding commerce, but also by keeping wages down to the lowest possible point in order to leave the largest possible margin available for the accumulation of capital.

Wages, then, in the new factory industries were kept low by competition and repression until about the middle of the nineteenth century, and a disproportionate share of the new wealth poured into the hands of employers, merchants, bankers, and the investing classes as a whole. The middle classes grew rapidly in numbers and in social influence and speedily became a powerful force in English political life; for though Parliament remained largely aristocratic in its actual composition until well after the middle of the century, after the Reform Act of 1832 Whigs and Tories alike had to govern the country mainly in accordance with middle-class economic ideas. The British Corn Laws were not finally repealed until 1846, but in the meantime, beginning with the Poor Law Act of 1834, there had been a steady stream of legislation reflecting the interests and economic doctrines of the new employing class. There were, indeed, Factory Acts such as those of 1833, 1844 and 1847 (the Ten Hours' Act) which granted some protection against excessive hours and insanitary conditions to the women and children employed under the factory system; but such Acts were still few and imperfectly enforced, and applied in any case only to the textile industries. Humanitarianism and sanitary legislation could not make great or steady progress until after the Reform Act of 1867 had extended the franchise to a considerable section of the urban working class.

In the meantime population grew apace and came to be more and more concentrated in the new industrial districts, so that the problems of sanitation and town government became more and more pressing. The rise of population itself was undoubtedly due far less to any actual increase in the birth-rate than to a decline in the death-rate, and especially in infant mortality, as medical science advanced and doctoring became more widely available. It certainly cannot be charged against the Industrial Revolution that it killed its victims more than the system which it replaced, but only that in the desire to get on quickly and in hatred of State intervention the new economic governing class was deplorably slow in equipping the new factory areas with even the rudiments of sanitation and municipal government. Panic on account of the cholera did lead to the passing of a Public Health Act in 1848, but this Act was hedged round with many restrictions and was allowed to lapse a decade later. Not until 1872 were Public Health services in the towns put on solid foundations, and not until 1888 was Great Britain equipped with representative Local Government bodies for the country districts as well as for the towns.

These deficiencies, however, in the structure of British social life did not prevent Great Britain from advancing fast in wealth and productivity or from winning for its industries easily the first place in the expanding markets of the world. It is easy to see why, under the conditions of the mid-nineteenth century, Free Trade suited British interests and *laissez-faire* seemed to the leaders of British industrial life the best of all possible systems. Far ahead of all rivals in the application of the new industrial methods, British capitalists were able to pick and choose among the forms of production, taking to themselves, without the need for any sort of protection, those which offered the highest prospects of profit, and leaving manufacturers in other countries to make the most of what was not worth their while. In cotton goods, in woollen goods, in the production of coal and iron, and in engineering and shipbuilding, in railway and locomotive construction, and in the arts of selling goods as well as of making them, British manufacturers and traders were well ahead of all their rivals; and with the triumph of steam over sail and metal over timber, Great Britain became predominant after the middle of the century in shipping and shipbuilding as well. British capitalism had the greatest abundance of free capital available for investment at home and abroad, the most developed system of banking and finance, and the most stable government in the world. In these circumstances Protection would have been of no use to the main body of British manufacturers, and was demanded only by agriculturists and by a few decaying and unprogressive industries. The wonder is not that the protective system was swept away but that it survived so long, when the interests of the commercial classes plainly demanded cheap food as well as cheap materials for industry.

Unhappy as the condition of the British workers was during the first half of the nineteenth century, and evil as were the sanitation and government of the growing industrial towns, the fact remains that on the whole the British industrial working class was ahead in its material standards of life of the urban population of either France or Germany. Both these countries, indeed, retained their peasant populations on the land, whereas in England the peasantry as a class had almost disappeared and the sufferings involved in their destruction had been prolonged and intense. Even in 1850 the English agricultural labourer was very badly off; and his poverty is a serious count in the indictment of the new industrial order. But the British skilled artisan and even the miner or the factory operative certainly had better wages and better material living standards than their Continental compeers, and working and living conditions in British mines and factories were, at their worst, no worse than comparable conditions abroad. The skilled artisans, however, were relatively much better off than the factory operatives, despite the fact that Great Britain's advantage in efficiency was mainly in the factory trades; for the supply of skilled labour was short in relation to the demand, while that of unskilled factory labour was abundant. The artisans were thus able to secure a share in the increased national wealth and prosperity much more easily than the less strongly organised and less articulate bodies of workers in the mining and factory districts. Relatively low wages in the mines and factories thus helped to enhance Great Britain's competitive advantage in the world market; and the very success of British export trade was used as an argument for keeping factory wages down. There was a constant demand for fresh capital in order to expand production, and before the days when joint-stock organisation had become the customary form for manufacturing industry there was no ready means of raising capital for it from any wide investing public. Manufacturers had then to rely largely on the accumulation of capital out of profits; and this caused them to regard the raising of wages as undesirable because it diverted badly needed resources from industrial expansion to "unproductive expenditure" on consumable goods. The new wealth of the factory districts, therefore, piled up disproportionately in the hands of the employing class, and wages, though they rose, remained low in relation to the rapidly rising productivity.

In the United States, on the other hand, wages were kept high from the first in the manufacturing areas by the shortage of labour, unskilled as well as skilled, in relation to the rapid growth of demand, and also because free land was available in the interior and in the far West. Employers were therefore compelled to offer the wage-earners sufficient inducements to remain in their service. This necessity of paying high wages reacted on commercial policy, stimulating the political movement for the protection of manufacturing industry and accentuating the already strong tendency towards Economic Nationalism. It has been estimated that in 1825 the average daily wage of a carpenter was 6s. in the United States, 4s. in England and 2s. 6d. in France, while that of a woollen weaver averaged 3s. 9d., 3s. and 2s. in the same three countries. No great accuracy attaches to such estimates, but they serve at any rate to indicate roughly relative wage-levels of the early nineteenth century.

To sum up, by the middle of the century Great Britain's economic life had been revolutionised by the advent of the railways and by the rapid spread of mechanical power in productive industry. Continental Europe was a long way behind Great Britain in these respects, but in Western Europe the great era of railway-building had already begun and the introduction of machinery was being greatly speeded up. The United States had developed enormously in wealth and population and was already in enjoyment of a relatively high standard of life. There, too, the railway age was coming in fast; and the opening up of the West was rapidly altering the economic balance of the country, isolating the Slave States and preparing the way for the outpouring of American foodstuffs into the world market. But cotton was still the principal American export, and the United States had not yet become the world's granary — much less the source of a large part of the world's supply of other primary products. American commercial policy, like that of continental Europe, was strongly Protectionist, and even in Great Britain the Free Trade era had barely begun — for the Repeal of the British Corn Laws in 1846 was only a stage in the adoption of Free Trade, and the structure of the Free Trade system was not completed until Gladstone's Budget of 1860. Even the Navigation Laws, which had been revised by Huskisson on the basis of " reciprocity " treaties in 1825, were not finally repealed until 1849. The true Free Trade era in Great Britain began only when British industry had already established its supremacy in the markets of the world.

VI

The Development of France and Germany

FREE Trade in wheat, when it came at length in 1846, by no means ruined either the British landlord or the British farmer, as the defenders of the Corn Laws had prophesied that it would. The removal of agricultural protection did bring about a considerable diversion of land from arable to pasture, and changed substantially the character of cultivation; but it caused no sudden inrush of foreign foodstuffs, and the expanding demand for milk, poultry, cheese, vegetables and fruit gave the farmer ample compensation for the loss of his privileged position as a grower of wheat. Moreover, the great prairie districts of the New World had not yet, in 1846, been effectively opened up, and not until the 'seventies did cheap wheat from America seriously menace the position of the British arable farmer. In the supply of meat the British farmer's advantage lasted longer still. The refrigerator ship was not introduced until the 'eighties, and even then it took time to develop the meat industry of the United States, the Argentine, Australia and New Zealand. In the long run Free Trade did hit British agriculture hard, but this effect was very long delayed. During the third quarter of the nineteenth century British agricultural rents moved steadily upwards despite the repeal of the Corn Laws, and both landlords and farmers profited much more from the increasing wealth of the country than they lost by the abandonment of the protective system.

Under these conditions Great Britain presented to the rest of the world the spectacle of a country flourishing exceedingly under Free Trade. Adam Smith's invectives against the " mercantile system " acquired fresh authority from the apparent benefits of taking his lessons to heart. The great German economist, Friedrich List, who had lived long in America, did indeed argue that Great Britain flourished under Free Trade only because its industries had been previously built up behind a high wall of Protection, and that other countries capable of manufacturing development should similarly protect their home producers until they had had time to become equally efficient. According to List, Free Trade was the right system for a country when once its industries had become fully grown, but their growth would need to be fostered by the State and foreign products should be kept out during their period of adolescence. List's doctrines, first enunciated in the 1840s, had great influence in America; but in Europe the object-lesson of British prosperity for some time set the tide flowing, if not towards Free Trade, at any rate towards less unfree trade. In the third quarter of the century both France and Germany on the whole lowered their tariffs; and the Cobden Treaty of 1860 between Great Britain and France was universally regarded as an outstanding victory of British economic ideas.

In the meantime, the new methods of production, of which Great Britain had been the pioneer, were gradually being adopted in other countries; but up to 1860 no other country had seriously begun to reproduce the essential character of the British industrial system or to challenge British pre-eminence in the world market. Great Britain's nearest rival in mining and manufacturing production was Belgium, which had been a separate State since the successful Revolution of 1830 had secured its dissociation from Holland. Belgian industrialists were in advance of the rest of continental Europe in applying the new productive techniques in textiles, in coal-mining and in the metal trades, and British capital played a considerable part in Belgian economic growth. But Belgium, highly industrialised though it had become, was too small to count as a dangerous rival to Great Britain save over a quite small area in Western Europe. The only two European countries which could have successfully challenged Great Britain in the world's markets were France and Germany; and in fact French economic development pursued a different course, while Germany hardly began until the latter part of the century to apply the new techniques of production. Until 1870 British supremacy in the world market remained practically unchallenged.

As we have seen, throughout the eighteenth century France had been economically as well as politically Great Britain's principal rival. France was then wealthier than Great Britain, though the wealth was even worse distributed, and the peasants in particular were ground down by intolerably heavy imposts in the interests of a practically functionless landed class. Up to the Industrial Revolution, French industry had been ahead of British in the use of complex machinery and in the development of large factories. But the burdens of the long war fell very heavily on the French economic system and prevented post-war France from either learning or applying the new techniques based on steam-power until long after they had become securely established in Great Britain. France emerged from the Napoleonic wars poor in capital and with a peasant class so firmly consolidated in its possession of the land as to put powerful obstacles in the way of the growth of an urban proletariat like that of Great Britain. France kept, indeed, its old supremacy in the silk industry and a wonderful talent for the small-scale production of goods of high quality and artistic finish. The French were great at wine-making and self-sufficient in agriculture, and the country soon became prosperous again as the effects of the war were left behind. But, both politically and economically, France was ill-equipped for rivalry with Great Britain in the world market. Coal supplies were small; and the great iron-ore resources of Lorraine were of little value until new methods of steel-making by the basic process which eliminates the phosphorus were introduced in the 1870s — and by that time Lorraine and its iron had passed from French to German control.

Under these circumstances the old causes of rivalry between France and Great Britain tended largely to disappear. French and British industry developed along different lines, and there was no likelihood that the French would effectively challenge the British manufacturers in the new forms of production for the world market. France came to be predominantly a country not only of peasant cultivators but also of small employers and master-craftsmen, rather than of factory owners and factory workers. The introduction of steam-power into French industry was very slow, and joint-stock organisation made relatively little progress except in banking and finance. Small-scale production in industry as well as in agriculture remained the basis of French economic life right up to 1914.

The French had, on account of this special structure of their economic system, the less reason for erecting high tariff barriers against cheap British goods, for French and British industries were in effect, for the most part, non-competitive. France, like Great Britain, remained Protectionist during the first half of the nineteenth century; but Free Trade doctrines, which had been first formulated in France by the Physiocrats in the previous century, were re-imported by French economists after the days of Adam Smith, and from 1848 onwards French fiscal policy became more liberal, largely under the influence of English ideas and English example. This tendency, however, was not to last. After the loss of Alsace-Lorraine in 1871 and the establishment of the Third Republic, Protectionism once more gained ground, and by 1892 France had reverted to a system of high Protection for industry, coupled with a corresponding Protection for the agricultural producers against the cheap foodstuffs which were flowing in from the New World. The only tariff system that could command national support in France was one devised in the interests of the peasants as well as of the industrialists. France chose, on the whole, to develop its home market in preference to export trade, and aimed at a balanced economic system that would reduce national dependence on either foodstuffs or manufactures from overseas.

This, of course, does not mean that France was of no account in the world market. The French had throughout the century which ended in 1914 an important and growing export trade, and bought large quantities of both capital goods and raw materials from abroad ; but French exports were largely specialised products commanding a market on account of taste and quality rather than of cheapness. There was little mass production and relatively little competition with either British or German industry. Only when Alsace-Lorraine had been regained in 1918 and the developed German industrialism of that area had been taken over by the French ironmasters did France become comparable with either Great Britain or Germany as a producer of iron and steel, or French economic policy come to be dominated largely by the interests of the heavy industries. French steel production had indeed been developing very fast in the years immediately before the First World War, but the Comité des Forges became the head and forefront of reaction and the leading influence in French economic policy only during and after the

War of 1914–1918. The most important French ventures in mass production, the Citroën and Renault motor works, also became important in the world market only after 1918.

In the first half of the nineteenth century Germany was even less able than France to compete with the developing industries of Great Britain. Divided politically into a large number of separate States, each with its own economic policy and its own Customs duties levied largely for revenue, Germany remained for the most part poor and economically undeveloped and made little attempt to adopt new productive techniques. The richer centres, such as Hamburg, throve by commerce rather than by industry, and Germany remained predominantly a country of small-scale handicrafts and domestic production. The German market was from the first of great importance to British industry and furnished the largest outlet in Europe for British goods; but only in the 1870s, after the consolidation of the German Empire, did the rivalry between Great Britain and Germany in the world market really begin.

Long before this challenge had become effective, the Germans had been slowly rousing themselves from their helplessly divided condition to become, under Prussian leadership, a great military power; and from the first the statesmen who controlled German policy realised that military strength must depend largely on economic development. German economic history immediately after the Napoleonic wars is bound up on the one hand with the reform of the agrarian system and on the other with the extension of Prussian influence through the making of liberal commercial treaties with the other German States. This policy led up to the initiation of the *Zollverein*, or Customs Union, in 1833; and the *Zollverein* was gradually extended until it covered, by 1852, nearly all the German States. The policy of removing internal restrictions on German commerce was meanwhile steadily pursued, and German Protectionism in relation to the outside world remained strictly moderate and was combined with a readiness to conclude liberal treaties with other countries. Even after the *Zollverein* had reached its appointed end in the political as well as economic unification of Germany, Protection for some time still remained very moderate — for Germany needed large quantities of imports in order to develop its economic life. But the severe trade depression of the later 'seventies changed the current of German opinion and led to an upward movement of tariffs, including the protection of agriculture as well as of industry. The landowning interests were too strongly entrenched in control of the State to submit to a protective system that left them out: the consequence was a compromise which was designed to consolidate Germany as a national commercial State with a wide range of manufactures within its borders, but at the same time maintaining a high level of agricultural production. The German tariff of 1879 was not high by modern standards, but a higher tariff was introduced in 1890 and one yet higher in 1902. German industry thus grew up during the closing decades of the nineteenth century behind a rising tariff wall under an economic system based on Friedrich List's doctrines of Economic Nationalism, but flouting his precepts by protecting agriculture.

To Great Britain Germany soon became a much more important rival than France, both because the German market had been previously of more importance to the British manufacturer and also because German industry developed along competitive lines with British, especially in the rapidly growing branches of production based on coal and iron. Germany, unlike France, had after 1871 ample resources for the building up of powerful industries of these types. German coal production expanded very fast, and in Lorraine and the Ruhr a great steel industry based on the newest methods of production grew rapidly in the 1870s and 1880s and challenged more and more successfully the position of British steel in the Continental markets.

In the metal industries, indeed, Great Britain now suffered from having been first in the field. In the earlier part of the nineteenth century the British had built up a great iron industry, in which they had easily taken the lead over all competitors. But from the 1850s came a series of new inventions which revolutionised the whole group of industries based on metal manufacture. In the 1850s the introduction of the Bessemer process cheapened enormously the production of steel — or rather led to the widespread use of a new product, mild steel or carbon iron, which had great advantages over iron for a wide range of uses, could be produced as cheaply as high-quality iron, and also wore longer and stood harder usage. This decisive invention made necessary the reconstruction of much of the plant of the old-established iron industry, as the new kind of steel rapidly displaced iron for one purpose after another. In the 1860s the introduction of the Siemens open-hearth process as an alternative to the Bessemer process made further reconstruction necessary, and this had not yet been completed when in the 1870s the new discoveries of Gilchrist-Thomas made possible the use of iron-ores with a high content of phosphorus and so stimulated the growth of German competition based on the phosphoric iron-ores of Lorraine. The Germans, coming late into the field, were able to equip themselves from the outset with plant of the most up-to-date types, whereas the depression of the later 'seventies, which fell with exceptional force on the metal trades, held back the reconstruction of the British iron and steel industry in accordance with the latest technical knowledge.

Nevertheless, Great Britain continued for some time to lead the world as a producer of steel. In the middle 'eighties British production was still more than twice that of Germany, and was still ahead of that of the United States; but in the 1890s the American production easily out-distanced the British, and early in the twentieth century Germany also went ahead of Great Britain. The American production, though it soon became by far the largest in the world, was of relatively little importance in the world market; for nearly the whole of the American output was absorbed in the enormous expansion of consumption in the United States itself. But the Germans, while they also consumed most of their steel at home, were able not only to dispense with a high proportion of their imports of British steel and engineering products but also to enter more and more into world competition with Great Britain in the steel and engineering trades.

German exports of a wide range of manufactured products grew extraordinarily fast during the closing decades of the nineteenth century, and at the same time British manufactured exports to Germany fell off sharply, as they had done earlier in the case of the United States in consequence of the growth of home production for the American market. But, even so, Germany, like the United States, remained an exceedingly important market for British goods. The place of the manufactures which Germany no longer needed to import was taken largely by British coal, which was imported in growing quantities into Western Germany owing to its high quality and the relative cheapness of sea-transport, which made it easier to move coal to Western Germany from British collieries near the coast than to bring coal west or north by a long land-haul from the inland German coalfields.

The metal industries thus came to be the principal field for British and German economic rivalry. In the textile industries Germany remained a long way behind Great Britain as an exporter; but in iron and steel German exports had come, before 1914, to exceed the

British in quantity. In the engineering trades, too, taken as a whole, the Germans were overhauling the British exporters extraordinarily fast, and were already, in the years immediately before 1914, not far behind them. Great Britain maintained its pre-eminence as an exporter of coal, but was being challenged by the Germans in precisely that group of industries in which the growth of world production was most rapid — the industries characteristic above all others of the mechanised and highly capitalised economy of the modern world. Moreover, the Germans had built up their remarkable position in the world market within a single generation and without the aid of any large colonial markets such as Great Britain enjoyed. German progress in wealth and trade was thus striking indeed, and it is not necessary to look beyond it for the main source of Anglo-German hostility and imperialist rivalry in the decade before 1914.

While, however, German and British industries had become rivals over a wide field in the markets of the world, internally the two economic systems were radically unlike. Germany had a protected home market, whereas Great Britain admitted imports freely from all other countries. Great Britain had large capital investments abroad on which the British economy received interest, largely in the form of goods, though a substantial part of the proceeds was reinvested abroad: Germany, on the other hand, was still a debtor country, borrowing capital from abroad, and using the borrowed money both for making foreign investments and for granting long credit to buyers. A further significant contrast between the two countries was that in Great Britain, in accordance with *laissez-faire* ideas, the State interfered as little as possible with industry and commerce, whereas in Germany industry had grown up with direct encouragement from the State and largely under State tutelage. The British railways were private and competitive, whereas the German railways were State-owned and State-administered. British banking and finance were largely internationalised in outlook, and fully as ready to provide money for financing transactions between foreigners as for British industry and trade, whereas German banking regarded itself definitely as the auxiliary of German productive and commercial development. Trusts and combines, though they existed in large numbers in Great Britain, were still frowned on by public opinion and secured no recognition from the law; but in Germany the organisation of industry into cartels and similar bodies was actively encouraged by the State, which actually participated in the Rhenish-Westphalian Coal Cartel. Germany had a large peasant population in the west and great feudal landed estates east of the Elbe. The German State protected agriculture as well as industry, whereas in Great Britain the peasantry had long disappeared and farming in all its forms was exposed to the full rigours of world competition. Above all, the temper of British business men, formed in the early part of the nineteenth century, was strongly individualistic; and British industrialism had an international outlook in the sense that the British producer thought of himself as concerned with the world market and took little account of political boundaries in shaping his economic policy. The temper of the German business man, on the other hand, was much more nationalistic: he was disposed to seek the realisation of his aims through collective action under the encouragement and protection of the national State.

This disposition to act collectively ministered to German success in the rapidly growing heavy industries, which responded more readily than the textile trades to methods of large-scale organisation. There was little advantage in making cotton mills or woollen mills very big; whereas technical changes in the metal trades were making larger and larger units of production indispensable for reducing costs, and were also creating the need for growing specialisation in the output of each particular factory. This involved not only the accumulation of capital in large masses — for which Great Britain was better equipped than Germany — but also a spirit of co-operation among the different firms in the same trade — and for this Great Britain was by no means so well equipped. Even so, right up to 1914 the British metal and engineering trades continued to make rapid progress ; but in Germany these trades went ahead faster still and commanded with every year a greater share in the total world market.

VII

The Growth of the United States

MEANWHILE, across the Atlantic, a country potentially far wealthier than any other, with the most fertile territory and the vastest natural resources in the world at its disposal, had been developing its economic life along lines radically different from those of Europe. During the earlier part of the nineteenth century the United States, despite a considerable growth of manufactures and an early resort to mechanical power for both production and transport, remained predominantly agricultural and imported manufactured goods from Great Britain and continental Europe in return for exports of foodstuffs and of raw materials such as tobacco — the leading commercial crop in the eighteenth century — indigo, rice and timber. The export of cotton became important at the very end of the eighteenth century, and from that time grew with astonishing speed. The export of wheat came much later and did not reach large dimensions until well after the middle of the nineteenth century. The chief exporters at this stage were still the planters of the Southern States, who used slave labour for the growing of crops suitable for large-scale production. The Northern States were peopled chiefly by farmers producing for their own subsistence or for the home market. Industries were, for the most part, on a small scale and were hampered in applying the new techniques of power production by the limitations of the domestic market. The future of the United States seemed, then, to lie less in production for export than in the growth of a balanced system of agricultural and industrial production, with the home market mainly in view.

Despite the vast growth in the scale of enterprise, the economic development of the United States has largely fulfilled this idea of internal self-sufficiency. The growth of the slave population of the Southern States was indeed bound up with the development of production for export, and at a later stage the huge interior was opened up largely as a source of supply of foodstuffs which could be profitably exported to Europe in exchange for manufactures — especially capital goods — and for such raw materials as are not found in sufficient abundance in the United States. But only in the cotton and tobacco districts did production for export ever play a dominant part in setting the course of economic policy. Save in these areas, the home market always remained the most important consideration. The battle between the North and South, finally fought out in the Civil War, was in effect a struggle not only between slave-owners and employers of free labour but also between Free Traders interested mainly in exports and Protectionists concerned chiefly with the home market. Its outcome made certain the dominance of Protectionism over the United States as a whole.

We have seen already that opinion in America had turned at an early stage towards Protectionism and that from 1816 to 1833 tariff duties on imported manufactures had been steadily increased. But during the next two decades, in view of the rapid opening-up of the country and of a growth of home demand which outran the capacity of the native manufacturers, this tendency was temporarily reversed, and tariffs were revised on the whole in a downward direction. From 1861, however, a new epoch of Protectionism began. The emergency duties levied largely for revenue during the Civil War were not removed, and in 1864 the average level of duties was three times as high as it had been under the Act of 1857. From this time onwards high and increasing Protection was the established basis of American fiscal policy.

Of course the development of industrialism in the United States is no more to be attributed to tariffs than its development in Great Britain is to Free Trade. Both countries, by reason of their natural resources, were obviously suited to industrial development, and both would have become great manufacturing powers whatever fiscal policy they had chosen to adopt. Great Britain, if it had clung to a Protectionist system, would probably have specialised much less in the great exporting industries, such as cotton, and would have maintained a larger rural population and a larger volume, in the long run, of agricultural production. The country as a whole would, in consequence, almost certainly, under the conditions which existed during the nineteenth century, have been less wealthy and its citizens would have acquired a much smaller quantity of overseas investments. One undoubted effect of Free Trade was to give a very great stimulus to the export of British capital. British influence in speeding up the industrialisation of other countries would thus have been lessened, and British capitalism would have been less international both in its dealings and in its economic outlook. But it is far harder to say what would have happened to the United States if Free Trade had been adopted as the basis of American economic policy. The growth of industries would probably have been slower, and that of agricultural production even faster, than they actually were; but industrial development would not have been stopped, although it might have taken somewhat different forms and the relative proportions of different industries might have been radically altered. The cost of living would certainly have been lower, but probably wages would have been lower too. Some purists in economic theory will doubtless claim that industry as a whole would have been more productive if some forms of production had not been fostered by Protection at the expense of others, and that America would have become a greater exporter of manufactures if Protection had not artificially raised the costs of production. This latter statement is certainly true, but the first is doubtful. For the United States, behind its high tariff wall, is the largest Free Trade area in the world, and with the growth of population the American market became big enough to afford full scope in almost every industry for the full economies of large-scale production. There are strong economic arguments against the maintenance of the high American tariff, now that the United States has become a great creditor country; but the familiar view that, in relatively small countries, tariffs lead to the fostering of industries for the products of which the home market is not large enough to afford adequate scope for efficient production, cannot be applied to the United States. The American tariff has been a great nuisance to Europe, but it does not follow that it has held back the growth of wealth and prosperity in the United States. Even if it could be shown that universal Free Trade is the system calculated to secure the greatest possible production of wealth over the world as a whole — which is doubtful — this would not prove that Free Trade must necessarily have the same effect within each separate country.

The stages by which the United States came to be the world's greatest producing area, though not the most important in foreign trade, are clearly marked by the growth of American population and output. The population of the United States doubled between 1860 and 1890, and trebled between 1860 and 1914. In successive decades from 1860 to 1920 it rose by 8 millions, 10 millions, 12 millions, 13 millions, 16 millions and 14 millions. In the same decades immigration accounted in round figures for 2 millions, 3 millions, 5 millions, 4 millions, 9 millions and 6 millions. The negro population rose from 4½ millions in 1860 to 10½ millions in 1920, but constituted by 1914 less than 10 per cent of the total. Immigrants, who were drawn in the earlier decades chiefly from Western Europe, came in the later decades much more largely from Southern and Eastern Europe, creating a problem of national assimilation which has not yet been wholly solved, though it became much less intractable when the door was closed to free migration after the First World War. Thereafter immigrants were admitted only under a quota system which discriminated according to the country of origin; and the total inflow was greatly reduced.

Even with a population of more than 150 millions in 1950, the United States remains a sparsely populated country. It has under 50 inhabitants to the square mile, compared with 194 in France, 466 in Western Germany, and about 750 in England and Wales. A considerable part of the population is still rural. Despite the rapid growth of industries, even in 1940 nearly 20 per cent of the total working population was still engaged in agriculture, forestry and fishing, as against less than 28 per cent in manufacture and mining, 5 per cent in construction, 6 per cent in transport and public utilities, 9 per cent in public employment and more than 32 per cent in trade, finance and other private services. In Great Britain, on the other hand, the proportion of the total working population engaged on the land in 1951 was well under 5 per cent, as against more than 37 per cent in manufacturing industry, 3⅔ per cent in mining, over 6 per cent in construction, 7½ per cent in transport and communications, 6 per cent in public services, 3½ per cent in the armed forces and 28 per cent in trade, finance and personal and professional services. In 1920 nearly half the total number of inhabitants in the United States were still classified as living in rural areas; but since then the growth of towns and industries has been astonishingly rapid. The urban population of the United States more than doubled between 1880 and 1900, and had nearly doubled again by the 1920s; whereas the rural population is still less than double what it was half a century ago.

Perhaps the clearest sign of the rapid industrialisation of the United States is the growth of coal production. In 1860 the total output of coal was under 15 million tons. This was doubled in the next decade, doubled again in the next and again in the next, reaching nearly 160 million tons in 1890. It was over 500 million tons in 1910, and over 600 million tons in 1920. Meanwhile, the output of pig-iron was trebled between 1850 and 1870, and multiplied five times between 1870 and 1900. It surpassed the British output in the early 'nineties, and was nearly three times as large as the British and twice as large as the German output in 1913. In steel, the United States was just behind Great Britain in the 1880s, but had four times as large an output in 1913. The value of American manufactures, according to the census returns, rose tenfold between 1860 and 1910. For the same period the total value of exports rose fivefold and that of imports more than fourfold. Up to the 1870s imports exceeded exports in value; but thereafter there was always a balance on the other side available for use in payment of shipping and financial services and in interest on capital borrowed from abroad. Right up to 1914 the Americans continued to import capital. The United States became a creditor nation only during the First World War.

Side by side with the advance in manufacturing industry went a rapid growth of agricultural production. The value of farm products, according to the census returns, more than doubled between 1870 and 1900, and rose more than fourfold between 1870 and 1910. Wheat output was nearly three times as great in 1880 as in 1860, and rose again rapidly in the 1890s, till it was nearly four times as large in 1910 as it had been half a century before. The number of cattle in the country more than doubled between 1860 and 1890, but thereafter ceased to grow as the free grazing area was reduced by the advance of arable cultivation. The number of pigs nearly doubled between 1860 and 1900, but showed thereafter a small decline. The production of wool, for which, rather than for their mutton, sheep are chiefly raised in the United States, grew more than fourfold between 1860 and 1910; while the cotton crop was between three and four times as large in 1910 as it had been fifty years before.

These great increases in agricultural output were achieved mainly under a system of small-scale farming, and the average agriculture holding was actually smaller in the 1930s than it had been in 1860. Nearly 60 per cent of the farms in the United States were of less than 100 acres, and only 18 per cent of more than 175 acres, but there had been a great advance in the use of farm machinery and also in the large-scale marketing of farm produce.

The great rise of American agricultural exports occurred in the latter part of the nineteenth century, as the new lands of the West were gradually opened up. The export of grain rose from 20 million bushels in 1860 to 293 million bushels in 1880; and it then nearly doubled again by the middle 'nineties. But thereafter, with increasing consumption at home, the surplus available for export fell off sharply. For the five principal cereals, it was 530 million bushels in 1897–8 and only 168 million bushels in 1913–14. Similarly, the export of meat rose from 46,000 tons in 1870 to 550,000 in 1880, only to fall off still more sharply as home consumption grew. After 1918 the United States fell to a position of declining importance as an exporter of foodstuffs, but greatly increased its importance as an exporter of a wide variety of manufactured goods; but raw cotton still retained its position as the most important single article of export.

Above all, the economic growth of the United States throughout the nineteenth century was that of a balanced productive system dependent relatively little on the outside world. In the twentieth century the U.S.A. came to be by far the largest exporting and importing country in the world, and even before the First World War it was second in exports and third in imports; but even of commodities of an exportable kind the Americans exported in the period between the wars less than 10 per cent of their total output, and in comparison with their total volume of production the proportion of exports was much smaller still. In comparison with Great Britain or Germany the United States was still — and still is to-day — a largely self-centred economic unit, despite its vast demands on world supplies of materials in which it is deficient in domestic resources — such as rubber and tin.

Nevertheless, the American scale of production and consumption is so vast that the United States became after 1914 a factor of enormous importance in world trade. The American impact on world conditions was therefore very great, and any fluctuation in the domestic demand, especially for raw materials, was liable to dislocate conditions in the world market; but the home trade is of so much greater importance to the Americans than their foreign commerce that right up to the Second World War American economic policy continued to be guided almost exclusively by domestic considerations. The consequences for other countries were sometimes most unfortunate, for although the Americans were in a position largely to ignore the rest of the world, other countries could not afford to ignore the United States. For a great creditor nation to maintain a large surplus of exports over imports is a very anomalous state of affairs, which can be sustained only if such a nation continually makes large overseas investments — or outright gifts — to restore the balance. But the Americans between the wars, after investing largely in Europe — especially in Germany — during the 1920s, ceased to follow this policy in the 1930s, and thus contributed greatly both to the coming of the world crisis and to its prolongation. The world's gold piled up in the United States — which did not need it — in payment for necessary imports; and other countries had to reduce their intake of American goods because of sheer inability to pay for them This situation reappeared in an exaggerated form after 1945, and disaster was averted only by the granting of huge free gifts to European countries under "Marshall Aid" and subsequently in the form of subsidies for the defence of the "free world" against Communism. Meanwhile, though some reductions were made in the American tariff, a policy of Protectionism remained in force; and even if it had not, the balance could hardly have been restored without a very great diversion of European purchases from America to non-dollar sources of supply.

The outstanding consequence of the enormous domestic wealth of the United States has been the establishment there of a higher standard of living for the main body of the people than exists in any other country. There remain great areas of comparative poverty, especially in the South, and the American standard of living is far from being uniform over the whole country. But a very large section of the American people, including most of the industrial workers, has undoubtedly a higher living standard than has ever been achieved elsewhere. In 1929, on the eve of the world depression, the American wage-level was in terms of purchasing power nearly twice as high as the British, and in terms of gold two and a half times as high, and the difference has since become substantially greater.

There is nothing new in this American superiority in wage-levels, so far as the more skilled workers are concerned. It was relatively almost as marked half a century ago as it is now. But it has spread in recent times to the less skilled, who used to be largely immigrants paid at much lower rates, but have now been absorbed and have learnt the arts of combination which used to be the prerogative of the skilled crafts. The disparity, moreover, is not confined to the working classes. It runs right up the social scale, creating in the United States a far vaster public with surplus income to spend on luxuries or to invest in future production than exists in any other country. The immensely rapid advance in the exploitation of American economic resources has meant throughout the history of the United States, despite recurrent crises, a prospect of very high profits for the successful business adventurer, and this prospect has bred in the American people a speculative temper of a kind that exists nowhere else in anything like the same degree. This temper has contributed greatly to the instability of the American business system and has exaggerated its repercussions on the rest of the world It has also prevented the development of any large body of Socialist opinion and has given even Trade Unionism in the United States a peculiarly individualistic turn. The American Socialist movement has been able to exert practically no influence on national policy, and the Trade Unions have shown no disposition to become the nucleus, as in Europe, of a Socialist political party, though they have become, since the world depression of the 1930s, increasingly active in pressing their political claims on the established parties. The absence of a class-conscious Socialist movement, comparable with those of Europe, has been characteristic of America right up to the present time.

This has not prevented a growing assimilation of

attitude between the American Trade Union movement and the non-Communist Trade Unions and Labour or Socialist Parties of Western Europe. But the policies common to these movements are those of the "Welfare State" as a promoter of social security and full employment rather than of any sort of Socialism. The United States has emerged into world politics as the great upholder of "free enterprise" in its capitalist forms, and has influenced other Western countries much more than it has been influenced by them.

VIII
Economic Imperialism

Up to the middle of the nineteenth century the new industrialism had taken root only in Western Europe and to a less extent in the United States. The Far East had been for centuries of importance to Europe as a source of supply for fine textile fabrics, luxury foodstuffs, and a few easily transportable materials; and with the rise of the cotton industry towards the end of the eighteenth century the Far East became important as a market also. Africa had been of account in the eighteenth century chiefly as a hunting-ground for slaves who could be caught or bought for sale in the American plantations, and its commercial importance dwindled after the suppression of the slave trade early in the nineteenth century. Canada was a sparsely populated agricultural country, supplying furs and timber, and becoming after 1840 of some account as a producer of grain for export. The only important Canadian industry was shipbuilding, and that died out after the introduction of steamships made of metal. Australia and New Zealand had between them a population of less than 200,000 and were of little economic account in world trade until after the gold discoveries of 1851, though the production of fine wool had begun. In South America, Brazil had been from early in the nineteenth century an important market, and there was a growing trade with the Argentine, Chile and Peru, but these countries were still in a rudimentary stage of economic growth until the latter end of the century.

Economic Imperialism

The half century before 1914 witnessed, besides the vast growth of the United States and the rapid industrial development of Great Britain and Germany, a swift extension of modern commercial and industrial methods to new countries. Japan, long almost isolated from world trade, not only opened its ports to foreign commerce but proceeded with extraordinary thoroughness and speed to equip itself with the productive techniques of the Western world. British capital covered India with a network of railways and began to develop Indian productive resources for the supply of Western needs — especially tea. The European occupation of Africa, previously confined to a few areas within easy reach of the coast, broadened out until practically the whole continent had been annexed by one or other of the European Powers. Russia, the granary of Europe, borrowed capital extensively from richer countries to build railways to link up its vast territories in Europe and Asia, and attempted, behind a very high tariff, to create modern industries of its own, largely under imported foreign management. New commodities, such as rubber and oil, immensely increased the economic importance of Malaya, the Dutch East Indies, Persia, Burma and Mexico. Commerce ceased to be confined to the old trade routes, and ocean-going ships carried everywhere the mingled blessings and curses of modern civilisation. A fever of railway-building seized on the world and provided vast openings for the investment of capital in the less developed countries. Trade, which in the earlier part of the nineteenth century had been mainly an exchange of goods for goods, often on most unequal terms, came to depend to a growing extent on the investment of capital abroad by citizens of the older countries. With this investment of capital came a startling revival of empire-building and a renewed tendency towards political interference by the more advanced nations in the affairs of the less developed. When a trader sells a man a shirt, that is an end of the transaction; but when a great industrial concern or a group of financiers builds, or finances the building of, a railway in a backward country, payment can be made only by instalments spread over a long period. In such circumstances the providers of the physical capital, or of the money spent on buying it, continue to take a lively interest in what is done with it. The capitalists of the investing countries come to have a stake in the debtor countries and to regard the existence of orderly and debt-honouring governments in these countries as one of the rights of property; and they are apt to call upon their own Governments for help if these rights are challenged, or if disturbed political conditions in the backward country upset their hopes of gain. Moreover, the Governments of the advanced countries themselves set to work to extend their colonial empires in search both of markets for their products and of assured sources for the supply of foodstuffs and raw materials for their use — or even mainly for the sake of preventing their rivals from occupying territories which they may want to control and develop at some future date.

The recrudescence of imperialism in the latter part of the nineteenth century was no merely causeless change of political attitude. It was based on a profound alteration in the economic relationships between the countries of the world. Richard Cobden and John Bright and most of their contemporaries in Great Britain had believed that it was only a matter of time for the white colonies to proclaim their independence and become sovereign States, as the United States had done in the previous century. Nor did they object to this; for they were convinced that trade would develop all the faster and more advantageously if no attempt were made to influence it by political pressure. In the native areas included within the British Empire, with the exception of India, the early Victorians took little interest; and on India many of them looked askance, as involving expensive responsibilities that were not worth while. Those who did value the Indian empire regarded it chiefly as a field for the expansion of the market for Lancashire cotton goods. The early Victorian capitalists looked at the world with the eyes of traders in finished consumable commodities, and their creed of *laissez-faire* followed logically from their economic ambitions.

But other countries, as they adopted the new industrialism, found themselves less fortunately placed than Great Britain. Their captains of industry found it hard to compete with the British in the open markets of the world, and they had no comparable colonial empires of their own. Just as they protected their own industries against British imports, so they set out to make such colonies as they had as far as possible closed markets for their own goods — and to get more colonies, in order to secure more protected markets and preferential fields for capital investment. British capitalism, confident in its industrial superiority and in its ability to lend capital more readily and on a larger scale than its rivals, felt for a long time no need to close its colonial territories to foreign products, even where it was in a position to impose its own terms; but the newer colonial empires of France and Germany grew up to a far greater extent as closed markets for the goods and capital of the metropolitan countries.

This does not mean that Great Britain was unaffected by the growth of imperialism. On the contrary, the British also set out to annex fresh territory and to build in every part of the Empire railways and other public undertakings which supplied profitable outlets both for British capital and for the products of the British industries making capital goods; nor did British economic activity stop short at the boundaries of the Empire. The Argentine was opened up mainly with British capital and

British machinery, and there was active British investment in China, as well as in India, and even in colonies belonging to other Powers, such as the Dutch East Indies.

This expansion of industrialism over almost the whole world is connected intimately with the growth of the metal trades, as closely as the earlier phases of the Industrial Revolution had been with the rise of the Lancashire cotton industry. In the second quarter of the nineteenth century coal, iron and engineering had laid the foundations of the new system of transport. Great Britain owed a great deal of its advantage at this stage to the abundance of its coal and to its possession of good supplies of iron-ore in close proximity to the coalfields. This second phase of the Industrial Revolution consolidated British economic supremacy. British engineering skill had built the main-line railways mainly between 1826 and the later 'forties, and thereafter the British engineers and contractors set out to use their acquired skill and experience in the profitable task of railway-building for the rest of the world. Great railway contractors such as Thomas Brassey, finding orders no longer plentiful at home, began to look further afield; but undeveloped countries could not afford to supply the capital for expensive railway projects, however great the prospects of economic expansion by their means might be. British capitalists, enriched by the profits of earlier ventures, could afford to lend the money as well as supply the skill. British capital, British technicians and British skilled labour undertook the task of equipping a large part of Western Europe, and later India and the Argentine, China and Africa, and many other parts of the world, with the new means of transport.

Railway construction occupies indeed a position of extraordinary significance in the evolution of modern capitalism. On the one hand it has been the means by which the hinterland of vast continents has been opened up to trade and settlement, and, jointly with the steamship, the instrument whereby the raw materials and the producing capacity of the New World, of Africa, and of the East have been made available for European use; and on the other hand it has largely influenced and determined both the structure of capitalist business and the growth of overseas investment as a means of hastening the spread of power production over a larger and larger part of the world.

The railway played an even more important part than the steamship in the promotion of international trade, for the steamship for the most part only enabled goods to be carried faster and in greater quantities along the familiar routes of commerce, whereas the railway multiplied many times over the area of the world open to commercial exploitation and settlement. Industrialism, before the coming of the railroads, could be hardly more than a fringe of smoke round the seaboards of even the most advanced countries. The railways industrialised, or at any rate commercialised, the interior as well. Above all else, they were the making of the United States as an advanced industrial nation.

But railway development was also of very great importance in its effects on the structure of the business system. The railway company, as it grew up in Great Britain in the second quarter of the nineteenth century, was modelled in its business structure on the earlier turnpike trusts and canal companies, which, like it, had been compelled to get special powers by private Acts of Parliament, because they needed the authority to invade private rights in order to construct their enterprises. But the railway company very soon developed on quite new and different lines. So large a mass of capital was needed to finance the host of projects for new railway construction that the money could be got only by making mass appeals and by drawing in large sections of the public who had been previously unused to industrial investment. The railway promoters appealed for capital to the rising middle classes of Great Britain, who needed new openings for the use of their money when the State had ceased to pile up war debts and there were few other fields open to savers who did not wish to take an active part in the use of their capital. In drawing in these classes, the railway promoters created the typical modern joint-stock concern with its widely diffused body of shareholders and stockholders, too numerous and too scattered to exercise any effective control over its conduct and interested in it solely from the financial point of view. The experience of railway flotations and railway stockholding prepared the way for a general acceptance of the joint-stock system and for the final concession of limited liability in all industries under the British Companies Act of 1855. There were of course other pioneers of joint-stock besides the railways — gas and water companies, for example — but in the evolution of the joint-stock system and in the widening of the investing public the railways played throughout the dominant part.

No less significant was the effect of railway development in internationalising the supply of capital. British overseas investment had indeed begun before the coming of the railways; there had been large private investments in the West Indian plantations and in North America during the eighteenth century. Moreover, after the Napoleonic wars there had been a boom in overseas issues, especially loans and investments in the South American States which had just thrown off the Spanish dominion and were looked to as expanding markets for British goods. But before the epoch of overseas railway construction there was not a great deal of investment of capital abroad except in Government loans or in purely private ventures such as the plantations of the West Indies. It was mainly through the building of railways overseas that British investors first learned to trust their money in foreign industrial ventures; and, in this respect too, what began with railways soon spread to other industries. The export of capital took a great and increasing place in the economic development of the modern world, and in this sphere, as in home investment, railway enterprise was the principal pioneer.

In this great movement of overseas investment Great Britain, as the only country with any large mass of surplus capital to invest, led the way. The rapid growth of British capacity to export goods provided the necessary resources, but exports could not develop to the full in a world much poorer than Britain unless British capitalists were prepared to lend to other countries the means of buying what they had to sell and were content to receive a deferred return as interest on their lendings. As we have seen, this overseas lending was largely confined in its early stages to public loans or to plantations; but after the coming of the railways it expanded into private industrial projects on a steadily increasing scale. In 1850 British capitalists had already perhaps £230 millions invested abroad, mainly in Government stocks, with a sprinkling of commercial and mining investment. By 1876, according to the most reliable estimates, the total had increased to about £1200 millions. Between 1860 and 1876 nearly £950 millions of new capital issues for overseas use can be traced in the London market. Rather more than half this total consisted of Government loans, including railway guarantees, and rather less than half of all other investments put together. The railways in the United States alone absorbed over £70 millions, and railway securities easily occupied the next place after public loans. It has been estimated that in 1914 British investors had at least £4000 millions invested abroad, and of this sum more than £1500 millions was in railway securities and £1000 millions in Government loans.

No other country had in 1914 even half so large a total overseas investment as Great Britain. France is estimated to have had about £1800 millions; Germany about £1200 millions; and the United States about £540 millions. The foreign investments of the United States were mainly in South and Central America; the French and German mainly in Europe and in their own colonies; but in all cases the total included a large mass of investments in railway securities, besides the proceeds of Government loans which had been devoted to the building of State-owned railway systems. France, outside its own colonies, had specialised chiefly in public loans and in the financing of the economic development of Russia; while Germany had distributed its investments about equally between Europe and the rest of the world, with a preponderance of fixed-interest-bearing securities. Only British investment was very widely spread over all countries and every type of bond and share, both public and private.

Undoubtedly this heavy investment of capital overseas greatly speeded up the economic growth of the more backward countries and stimulated in the more developed countries the expansion of the industries producing capital goods. It was indeed largely a result of the concentration of income in the hands of the richer sections of the community, for this both increased savings and limited the home market for consumers' goods, and thus provided an incentive to the active capitalists and financiers to be always on the look-out for fresh markets and fields for investment abroad in order to absorb the growing productivity of capitalist industry and the larger and larger masses of capital looking for profitable outlets. If wages had risen faster in the older countries, the aggregate increase of wealth in the world as a whole might possibly have been slower and the industrialisation of the less advanced areas would probably have been delayed, but

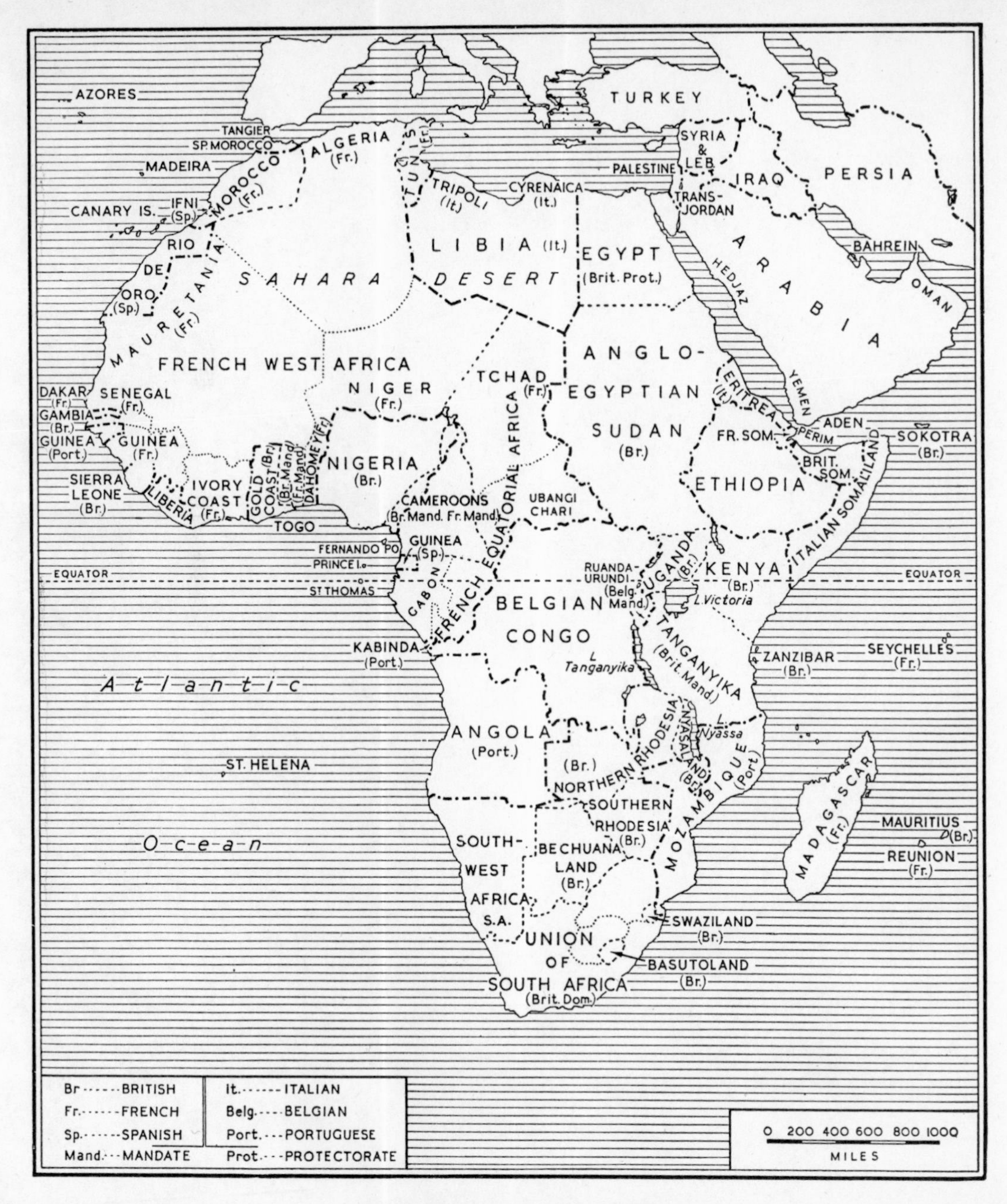

THE PARTITION OF AFRICA

there would have been a better diffusion of wealth in the developed countries. There would also have been less international rivalry, less imperialism and subjection of the weaker peoples, and less sowing of the seeds of war.

Yet, obviously, it is in itself a good thing for the richer and better-equipped countries to help on the development of the less advanced. Obviously, it would have been in every way better if this could have been done without either subjecting the borrowers to the political control of the lenders or involving the lending countries in quarrelling with one another about their rights to help in the expansion of the new industrialism. But, as the world was, the less advanced countries became, not so much willing borrowers from the more advanced, as recipients of loans and investments which were thrust upon them even against their wills and were applied to such purposes as suited the needs of the lending rather than of the debtor countries. Investment developed as a means of finding markets and raw materials and foodstuffs needed by the advanced countries, and was uninfluenced by considerations of the well-being of the peoples among whom it was made. Of course, it often raised the national incomes of the borrowing countries; but that was incidental only, and against this has to be set its effect in breaking up the old ways of living without providing any substitute pattern of culture adjusted to local needs. Moreover, the advanced countries were continually squabbling for the rights of their national capitalists to exploit the backward countries' resources. The enterprises set up in the less developed countries were often not only financed by alien capital and managed by alien technicians and supervisors but also conducted under alien control by companies registered and administered in the lending country. The white workers received salaries out of all relation to native incomes; and usually no attempt was made to train native workers for the more skilled tasks.

The profits of the enterprises were remitted home to the alien owners; and the countries in which the enterprises were carried on, unless they were recognised as fully civilised nations, had to submit to alien policing and often even to annexation, either open or disguised under the form of a protectorate or a mandate. The native inhabitants became in effect sources of man-power for the less skilled tasks under alien capitalists; and in many areas steps were taken to force reluctant tribesmen to supply labour to man the white man's mines and plantations. In other areas, such as Malaya, mass importation of workers from other backward countries changed the make-up of the local populations and created vast insoluble political problems of mixed societies. In some cases, a large part of the tax revenue of the backward countries came to be earmarked as security for the payment of interest on the alien capital. The capitalist world, in the latter part of the nineteenth century, became far less tolerant of uncivilised peoples and even of peoples backward in relation to Western standards of economic progress. While Europe was asserting within its own borders the rights of nationality and self-determination, it was also denying the right of non-European peoples to abstain from using to the full, according to Western notions, the potential wealth of their lands and their labour power, and was claiming the right to enforce the development of any territory inhabited by less civilised peoples, as part of the civilising mission of the white races.

Of course, from the standpoint of the capitalists in the advanced countries, with their faith in the virtues of large-scale production, there were reasonable arguments in support of this attitude. Modern capitalist industrialism could develop only if it could find both expanding markets for its products and larger and larger supplies of foodstuffs and raw materials which it could receive in exchange for them. It needed not only the produce of the prairie lands of America and the ranches of Australia, where there were relatively few natives to be dispossessed, but also that of tropical Africa, rubber and tin from Malaya and the Dutch East Indies, and a host of other commodities from countries already thickly populated by native inhabitants who would not and could not produce enough to meet the needs of the advanced countries except under the stimulus of white intervention. Why, asked the European capitalist, should these native populations be allowed to ignore the vast economic opportunities of the regions in which they dwelt? Their own standards of wealth and civilisation could rise only if they were taught how to use the resources lying ready to their hands; and only the white man could teach them. That was the white man's mission — a mission, as he saw it, of civilisation for the world as well as of enrichment for himself, a mission necessary in the interests of the progress of industrialism — which was assumed to be good. National self-determination, according to this view, could hold good only for peoples who had their eyes sufficiently open to the economic main chance. A sentimental regard for the cultural traditions and ways of living of the more primitive peoples must not be allowed to stay the civilising march of the capitalist industrial system.

But, unhappily, the white men did not march on their civilising mission either as a united army or with any notion of human equality or brotherhood in their minds. Even those who "got on well with the natives" commonly had a contempt for them and regarded their institutions without respect. Moreover, the white men disputed and even fought one another for the right to exploit the less developed regions of the earth. The partition of Africa was accomplished without actual war between the great Powers, which divided up practically the whole continent, but not without recurrent threats of war. In 1918 the colonial empire of Germany was parcelled out among the victors, and though the form of annexation was hidden under the cloak of the mandatory system and each annexing Power pledged itself to administer its mandated territories in the interests of their inhabitants, in effect most of the mandated areas were virtually added to the empires of the victorious Allies. One thing, indeed, was secured — the open door in these areas for the commerce of all nations — but with that exception the mandatory system differed little from positive annexation. Only after the rise of the Soviet Union and the development of native nationalism, which was greatly stimulated by the Second World War, did the older notions of imperialism go out of fashion ; and even then they died hard, especially in the French colonies, but also in Malaya and in East and Central Africa.

The root of the problem lay in the need of the developed countries for ever-expanding markets and sources of supply to keep their industries at work and their peoples fed. It is not in the nature of modern industrialism to stand still. It must either grow or decay, and under the conditions of the nineteenth century it had, in order to grow, to find markets for its products largely outside its own borders — except where, as in the United States, its home population was being reinforced by a stream of immigrants. Especially in Great Britain and Germany, industrialism grew up, not as a balanced system of production and consumption, but as a development of specialised production of certain classes of machine-made goods made largely out of imported raw materials — and under conditions which necessitated the importation of large quantities of foodstuffs as well. Any system of this sort must sell abroad in order to buy, and can raise the standard of living at home only by selling more and more of its products abroad. It must, moreover, if it is to have more to sell, assure itself of a constantly growing supply of necessary materials. This was much less true of France than of either Great Britain or Germany, and it has been still less true of the United States, with its vaster territory and its more balanced economic development of industry and agriculture. But it was broadly true of all the great empire-building countries. The inevitable result appeared in the growth of Economic Imperialism and in the rivalries of the great Powers for the effective possession of sources of supply as well as of expanding markets. The struggle for oil furnishes an outstanding example.

In sum, the latter half of the nineteenth century was marked by the development of a new kind of Economic Imperialism. Between 1884 and 1900 the territory of the British Empire was increased by more than 3·7 million square miles, containing more than 57 million people. France annexed 3½ million square miles, with more than 36 million inhabitants; and Germany, much less favourably placed, built up, chiefly in Africa, a colonial empire of over a million square miles, with nearly 17 million inhabitants. The United States took over Cuba, the Philippines, Hawaii and Alaska. Italy followed France and Great Britain into Northern Africa. Russia and Great Britain squabbled over Persia and intrigued in Afghanistan and the States of Central Asia. France, Spain and Germany fell out in Morocco. Belgium, under Leopold, attempted to develop the Congo on lines which shocked the conscience even of an imperialist world. In 1914 it was very nearly true that there was no territory left on the face of the earth which had not been appropriated or at least dominated by one or another of the "civilised Powers". The great exception was China, which had proved too tough a nut for even modern capitalism to crack: and China, because it could not be partitioned, had found itself at the mercy of the intrigues and rivalries of the great Powers. All the world over, Economic Imperialism had become a dominant force in world politics, and behind it loomed the ever-growing threat of war.

All the same, it is an error to interpret the imperialist tendencies of the nineteenth and twentieth centuries entirely in economic terms. Important as the economic factors of course were, they did not stand alone: side by side with them the old militaristic drives towards imperialist expansion persisted, and in certain countries the economic forces were fully as much instruments of State policy as influences impelling their States towards new conquests of potential economic value. For example, as we shall see in a later chapter, the great expansion of Czarist Russia in Asia certainly cannot be accounted for by the pressure of Russian capitalists for markets or sources of raw material or fields for the investment of surplus capital. Capitalism in Russia was not nearly a strong enough force to exert a preponderant influence, and Russia's drive in the East is to be explained much more in terms of militaristic power motives than of economic inducements. Nor can Germany's imperialism really be explained in exclusively economic terms. In Germany, the interconnection between the forces of militarism and capitalism was very much more complicated than it was in Czarist Russia, but it can hardly be disputed that the German drive for supremacy in Central and Eastern Europe, though it largely used economic means, was inspired fully as much by nationalist and militarist sentiment as by the search for markets. Even in the case of Africa the partition, though accounted for partly by economic inducements, was speeded up and universalised by the competitive prestige-seeking of the European Powers. One act of annexation led to another, not so much because there were real economic gains in prospect as because each participant in the scramble felt that it would lose " face " if it were behindhand with its rivals in acquiring additional territories. There were strong reasons why the capitalist system of the later nineteenth century turned away from the pacific courses of Cobdenism to policies resting on domestic Protection and the attempt to monopolise colonial markets, materials and fields of investment; but these economic forces did not operate in isolation from the political forces, which cannot be correctly represented as simply derivative or secondary. Imperialism is a very much older thing than capitalism, and although in the nineteenth century it took on new forms, deeply affected by changes in what Marx called " the powers of production ", the old lusts for power, the old militaristic impulses affecting whole nations and particularly their ruling classes, did not cease to operate: they were merely reinforced when monopolist capitalism became the ally or the auxiliary of militant expansionism, as it did in Japan as well as in Germany. Even in Great Britain it was certainly not from economic motives only that Disraeli caused Queen Victoria to be proclaimed Empress of India. Nor was the new imperialism at all welcome to important sections of the British capitalist classes. The new imperialism was not identical with the old, but it is fully as important to recognise its continuity as to draw attention to the way in which it was affected by the growth in the scale of economic enterprise and by the drive to find markets and materials and scope for the investment of surplus capital outside the older countries.

IX

The Far East

IN the course of the eighteenth century the British had driven the French out of India, and the British East India Company had grown from a corporation of traders into the government of a great empire. Great Britain had thus secured for its merchants by far the largest share in the available trade with the Far East. The East India Company controlled the trade with China as well as with India, and British merchants were able to build up a great position as middlemen with continental Europe in Far Eastern products. With the introduction of tea-drinking as a habit among larger and larger sections of the people, the China trade acquired a new importance, and after the rise of the cotton industry in England, India and China both became vitally important markets for British manufactures. Trade with India became less like open rapine and more a real exchange of goods ; but the native cotton industry of India, based on domestic spinning and on the handloom, suffered disastrously from the competition of the machine-made cloths of Lancashire.

As the nineteenth century advanced, the Far Eastern market grew steadily in importance, and India became a field for the large-scale investment of British capital as well as for the export of Lancashire's piece goods. Indian railways, irrigation works and other public enterprises were constructed mainly with capital borrowed from Great Britain and with capital goods made by British engineers. The China trade also grew in size and value, especially after the Opium War of 1840–42 had forced the Chinese to open the interior to foreign trade. Hong Kong, annexed in 1842, became the great depot for the British trade with Southern China, and the Chinese were compelled to open Shanghai and three other ports to British commerce, in addition to Canton, through which alone trade with Europe had previously been allowed. Great Britain forced China to admit Indian opium, and soon, in conjunction with the other Western Powers, imposed on the Chinese Government both acceptance of the rights of extra-territoriality for European and American nationals and limitation of the Customs tariff to a maximum rate of 5 per cent *ad valorem*. In 1853 the Americans, under Perry, forced open to Western products the closed markets of Japan; and this triumph of civilisation was followed by the American-Japanese commercial treaty of 1858 and by similar treaties between Japan and the other Western Powers. Japan, as well as China, had to accept a limitation of its Customs tariff to 5 per cent and to grant foreigners special privileges in its markets.

But whereas China, even after the opening and extension of trade with the West, remained in its own life almost unaffected by Western influences, the impact of Western ideas on Japan had very different results. Japan had long been the home of a culture largely not its own but borrowed from China; but from the Revolution of 1867 the Japanese set themselves, under new bureaucratic rulers, to imitate the West both in military and naval equipment and in methods of economic enterprise. With extraordinary thoroughness and imitative competence, they set to work to learn the techniques of machine production and to apply in their own country the methods of Western commerce and finance, but without changing the theocratic and authoritarian basis of their State or accepting the *laissez-faire* gospel of Western capitalism. Japanese capitalism grew up under State tutelage and as the auxiliary of the aims of the governing military caste. By stages the Japanese drove the foreign merchants out of the points of vantage for the conduct of overseas trade. They introduced Western banking institutions, at first mainly in imitation of the United States but later more extensively on European models. The Bank of Japan was founded in 1882 as a Central Bank with a monopoly of note issue. The currency, previously much inflated, was reformed and made convertible into silver, and after a phase of bimetallism Japan finally came over to the gold standard in 1897, using the proceeds of the indemnity exacted at the end of the Sino-Japanese War as the means of building up the necessary reserve of gold.

In the meantime, the war with China had afforded the Japanese the chance of displaying their military prowess, which was to be shown still more formidably in the Russo-Japanese War of 1904–5. Military success secured the recognition of Japan as a World Power by the great Western countries, and its new status was consolidated by the alliance with Great Britain concluded in 1902. At the same time, Japan's rulers modernised the industrial system, developing the production of iron and steel and engineering goods as well as of textiles, and seeking to build up an export market in China and the other countries of the Far East, with the aid of the cheap labour which Japanese industry was able to command. With a narrow and infertile territory and a rapidly growing population, Japan felt even more strongly than the Western countries the impulsion towards a policy of militant imperialist expansion. The Japanese occupied and subsequently annexed Korea, forced their way into sparsely populated Manchuria, and became masters of its rich economic resources. After 1905 Japan replaced Russia as the leading Power in North-East Asia.

While Japan was thus striding forward in the mastery of the arts of the West, an undignified scramble was in progress among the European Powers for the extension of their spheres of influence in China. It was widely believed that the old, unwieldy Chinese Empire was breaking up and that the problem of openings for trade and investment would in the end be settled by the piecemeal annexation of Chinese territory by the leading Powers. Indeed this process had already begun on a small scale. The British had instituted it when they annexed Hong Kong, and it had been continued when the French extended their Empire in Indo-China, when the British seized Upper Burma, and when the Russians descended on Manchuria in their quest for an ice-free port in the East. The United States, having taken the Philippines from Spain at the close of the Spanish-American War, had also become more closely concerned in the Chinese question; but American policy, unlike that of the European Powers, favoured the "Open Door" for the commerce of all nations, and on the whole American influence in the dealings of the West with the unfortunate Chinese was at this stage a moderating factor. It was largely owing to the Americans that the idea of partitioning China between the European Powers and Japan had to be given up. It had never been really workable. China was too vast and too densely populated a country for the annexation of the main part of its territory to be a possible policy for the Western Powers.

Even the Japanese discovered this, despite the ability of their armies to live on the country. It was possible to occupy large areas, but only to hold the main centres; the Japanese writ, even at the height of the penetration, never ran in the interior beyond the garrison centres and the communication lines. Outlying areas, such as Manchuria, could be effectively subdued and held, at least for a time; but China was tough and remained finally unassimilated.

Where Japan was to fail, the European Powers, whose

forces could not live on the country, could not hope to succeed, even if they had been able to agree among themselves on a concerted plan of spheres of influence — which they were quite unable to do. Indeed, the history of China during the decades before 1914 is mainly the record of an endless scramble for railway and other concessions by the Western Powers, and of the mortgaging of more and more of Chinese internal revenues for the service of external loans. As the idea of partitioning the country was abandoned, there was a growing tendency for the Powers to act in concert, and this finally led up to the Six-Power Consortium of 1912, which set out to put Chinese finances in order for the benefit of foreign creditors and investors. Great Britain, the United States, France, Germany, Japan and Russia were all parties at this stage to the Consortium; but in 1913 President Wilson, objecting to the proposed drastic interference with Chinese internal affairs, caused the United States to withdraw. Germany was practically eliminated as a result of the war, Russia was for the moment eclipsed; and the Consortium fell to pieces.

China, meanwhile, had been passing through a series of revolutions, and, hampered by foreign debt and intervention and by foreign control of Customs policy, was unable to establish an enduring government over the whole country. Japan used the opportunity presented by the first European War to extend its influence and to exact arbitrary terms from the Chinese, and later profited by the Russian Revolution further to extend its control in Manchuria and Northern China. Great Britain, concerned mainly with the South and the Yangtse Valley, cared little what happened in the North, and as French interests were also mainly in the South, Japan got more and more of a free hand in Manchuria and in the Shantung Peninsula, where the Japanese had inherited the concessions seized from Germany during the First World War.

China had thus been for many years before 1914 the

meeting-place and chief quarrelling ground of all the great imperialist Powers. After the effective partitioning of Africa had been completed, China was the one great territory in the world easily open to new imperialist aggression. European capitalism helped to provide China with railways and thus in some measure to prepare the way for consolidation under a single government after the Revolution of 1912. But subsequent history has shown that it is a good deal easier to establish a central government in China than to maintain its authority. It has still to be seen whether Chinese Communism will succeed where previous revolutions have failed.

Amid the unhealthy manifestations of economic imperialism, the industrialisation of the Far East was effectively begun; and, especially during and after the First World War, Far Eastern industries began seriously to threaten the supremacy of Western products in the Eastern markets. Japan, as we saw, was the pioneer in this process of industrialisation; but after 1914 it spread in both India and parts of China, and during the Second World War there were further big developments in India, in the heavy industries as well as in the manufacture of cotton goods. Moreover India, out of the proceeds of war exports, was able to repay the capital belonging to British investors, and to accumulate large sterling balances.

The competitive power of Japanese industry in foreign markets was based from the first on a plentiful supply of cheap labour; but even with its aid Japan had not become, until after 1914, a really important competitor, outside its own home market, of the European exporter. By Western standards Japanese labour and techniques of production were still up to that time at a low standard of efficiency, and Japanese industry had no advantage in total costs over the Western countries, despite their much higher wage-levels. Lancashire, for example, was fully capable, up to 1914, of meeting the competition of the

Japanese exporters of cotton goods.

The First World War, however, by interrupting the supply of European goods to Eastern markets, gave the Japanese their opportunity. Japan's exports rose sharply, and at the same time the efficiency of Japanese production was considerably improved. Meanwhile, the same causes as were speeding-up the growth of industry in Japan were leading to a parallel rise of the factory system in both India and China, where labour could be got at an even cheaper rate. As Japanese industrialism developed, wages in Japan rose fairly fast, though they still remained exceedingly low by European standards. Before long, Japanese employers began to complain of the competition of the cheaper labour of India and China, and Japanese capitalists started factories in China or Korea or imported Korean workers in order to get the benefit of labour at a lower wage. On the whole, however, the advance in Japanese industrial efficiency more than kept pace with the rise in wages, and as costs had risen in Great Britain and the other European countries Japanese competition with their exports became much more effective, especially in the Eastern markets.

Although industrialism was thus making a beginning after 1914 in India and China as well as in Japan, it has even now advanced in both these countries only a very little way. The overwhelming majority of the people in India and China are still employed on or about the land, and even manufacturing production, outside a few centres, still largely takes the form of handicraft. In China, for example, the quantity of cotton goods produced in the factories is still small in relation to the amount produced on handlooms. In India, too, even apart from the effects of Gandhi's propaganda, the handloom still supplies the needs of a large part of the rural population. It is still in spinning rather than in weaving that the greatest advances in factory production have been made.

This continued activity of handloom production has not, however, prevented the competition of Indian and Chinese as well as of Japanese factories from having been a very serious matter for the exporters of the Western countries, and, above all, of Great Britain. The greater part of Lancashire's former markets in the Far East has certainly been lost for ever to the cotton industries of Japan, China and India. Undoubtedly recent changes in industrial techniques have reduced the comparative advantages of the more advanced countries. The new automatic machines diminish the need for skilled labour and make it easier for the less strenuous and less skilled labour of the Eastern peoples to be used. The real reason why the factory system in the Far East did not advance even faster than it did between the wars was that the Far Eastern countries could not find the capital for more rapid development.

Moreover, the economic difficulties of the Far East were greatly accentuated between the wars by the fall in the value of silver. This decreased enormously the external purchasing power of countries such as China, which remained upon a silver standard. Japan, being on the gold standard, had to sell its goods abroad at prices measured in gold, and this meant asking the Chinese buyer a very high price in terms of silver. The Japanese merchants, with Government aid, tried to meet the situation by cutting their prices, and this of course reacted still further on the position of exporters in the Western countries, and, above all, in those which remained on the gold standard.

Clearly, the growth of industry based on modern power production in the less developed parts of the world is still only in its very early stages and is destined to exert a steadily increasing influence on the world economic situation. There is no inherent reason why, *in the long run*, both China and India should not do what Russia has achieved under its successive Five-Year Plans — that is, carry through a thorough-going reconstruction of their entire economic systems, including agriculture as well as industry, on lines of huge-scale collective organisation based on the use of mechanical power in its most developed forms. There are, however, *in the short run*, insuperable obstacles in the way. It was difficult enough for Soviet Russia to abstract, at the expense of the low standard of life of the great mass of the people, enough capital to finance the ambitious schemes of industrial reorganisation on which the Communist Party embarked. But Russia had, from this standpoint, the great advantage of being thinly populated in comparison with the countries of the Far East. For India and for China, the density of population, the very small size of the crowded peasant holdings, and the extreme poverty of the people put even greater difficulties in the way of any comprehensive plan of economic development out of their own resources.

At the end of the Second World War, Burma, Malaya, the Dutch Indies and Indo-China, all overrun during the war by the Japanese, were handed back to their European rulers when Japan surrendered; but in none of them, except Malaya, was there any real possibility of a return to the old system of colonial exploitation. Burma was given its independence along with India, and became a prey to civil war. War was also waged in Indonesia before the Dutch were compelled to accept an independent Indonesian Republic in union with the Dutch Crown. In Indo-China the French became involved in a colonial war of which no end is even now (1952) in sight. Even in Malaya, where imperial rule could be reinstated because there was no national unity between the Chinese and the Malay inhabitants, jungle warfare has continued unsuppressed. These struggles have restricted economic development, both directly and because they have made South-East Asia an obviously unsafe field for the investment of foreign capital. In India, too, development has slowed down, largely because the rapid increase in population has absorbed the resources of the country in the fight against sheer famine, but also because the uneasy relations between India and Pakistan have diverted to military uses funds that are sorely needed for measures designed to increase productivity and to bring more land into use.

Japan, put temporarily out of the world market and retarded in economic development by defeat in war, is now again emerging, under American tutelage, as a large-scale exporter, especially of textile goods. But even Japan, though far more highly developed than any other Asiatic country, is by no means fully industrialised by Western standards. Agriculture, including the cultivation of the silkworm, still provides the basis of living for most of the Japanese people. During the world depression of the 1930s the Japanese made great efforts to capture markets from the Western countries with a wide range of cheap manufactured goods — from textiles to bicycles and electrical gadgets. A large part of this trade was lost as a result of the war; but great efforts are now being made to regain it. Indeed, the Japanese are too crowded together to live tolerably without a great export trade. Their agricultural holdings are mostly very small — 70 per cent of the farms being of less than 2½ acres — and the country is poor in raw materials as well as in cultivable land. Japanese industrialism has been at all stages a remarkable *tour de force*; and behind it has been the sheer need to eke out scanty resources for the supply of a rapidly increasing population.

X

The Emergence of Russia

RUSSIA, vast and remote, lay, for the greater part of the two centuries dealt with in this book, mainly outside the range of the agricultural and industrial revolutions which transformed Western Europe and the United States. Till 1861 the people of Russia were largely serfs — to all intents and purposes the property of the landowning classes. There were industrial developments in spite of this; but they were largely either in State factories for munition-making or in factories carried on by landowners with serf labour. The free sector of industry was small, and could hardly grow because of the narrow limitations of the market. The serfs had hardly any purchasing power: the wealthy wanted imported luxuries rather than native products. After the emancipation of the serfs in 1861, industrial growth remained slow. The peasants, still largely tied to the land, were weighed down by heavy taxes for compensation to the landowners, and for some time could buy little more than before. But agricultural productivity soon showed a marked increase; active railway-building began, and presently there was an influx of foreign capital, and new industries were started up with the aid of foreign technicians and managers. The consumption of raw cotton rose from 31,000 tons in 1861 to 147,000 in 1881 and 212,000 in 1901: production of pig-iron was 320,000 tons in 1861, and nearly 3 million tons in 1901.

Over the same period there was a great expansion of

the Russian State. This indeed had been going on for centuries. Vast territories had been subjected to the Muscovite rule under Ivan the Terrible during the sixteenth century; and during the first half of the seventeenth the advance across Siberia was continued apace. Yakutsk, in north-east Siberia, was founded in 1632, and in the 1640s Russian adventurers crossed the Behring Straits to Alaska. The Russians also moved into the Amur Valley, but had to retreat before the Chinese. In Europe, the Ukraine was annexed after the Polish War of 1654–67; and during the first quarter of the eighteenth century, under Peter the Great, Russia secured a western outlet to the Baltic after defeating the Swedes. At the Peace of Nystadt (1721) Sweden ceded Livonia, Estonia, Karelia, and part of south-eastern Finland. Peter the Great set out to make Russia a great Western Power; but he also extended Russian influence in the East, attempting to conquer Khiva and Bokhara and to establish direct trade relations with India and also making war on Persia and securing access to the Caspian Sea. This last, however, was lost after Peter's death. In the second half of the eighteenth century came the three successive partitions of Poland which gave the Russians Lithuania, Courland, and the rest of the Ukraine, and also the Russo-Turkish wars which carried Russian rule to the Crimea and to the northern coast of the Black Sea. Sevastopol was founded as a great naval port, and a little later Odessa as a trading centre. During the Napoleonic wars Alexander I annexed Georgia, and in the 1820s a war against Persia ended in the Russian acquisition of Erivan and other areas in the Caucasus and in Russian domination of the Caspian Sea. Immediately afterwards renewed war with Turkey gave the Russians the mouth of the Danube and more Caucasian possessions. Moldavia and Wallachia, as autonomous areas, passed under Russian influence. But these advances into the Near East roused

Great Britain and France to opposition; and as an outcome of the Crimean War the Russians had to withdraw from the Danube and to surrender the right to maintain a fleet in the Black Sea. They renewed their drive in the Turkish War of 1877; but again Great Britain and France barred the way, and at the Congress of Berlin in the following year the Russians had to accept a check to their ambitions in the Near East.

The effect of these set-backs was to drive Russian imperialism farther east. Already, in 1858, China had ceded the Amur region, and two years later the Maritime Provinces, where Vladivostok was founded in 1860 as a Russian stronghold on the Pacific. In the 1870s and 1880s the Russians completed their conquest of the Caucasus and pressed on to the east of the Caspian to the frontiers of Persia and Afghanistan. Meanwhile, over the vast Asiatic territory of the Russian Empire, russification and colonisation had been proceeding side by side. Between 1823 and 1898 nearly a million exiles and voluntary sharers in their exile entered Siberia; and after the abolition of serfdom there was in addition a considerable movement of free settlers, which became much greater after 1900.

Thus the Russians, during the nineteenth century as well as earlier, were even more ambitious empire-builders than the nations of the West. But their empire-building was different, both in that it was predominantly military, with economic matters taking second place, and because it took the form of an extension of the continuous land area under Russian rule and of persistent attempts at russification of the conquered peoples. With certain notable exceptions, such as Poles and Finns in the West and the Mahometan peoples in Central Asia, the inhabitants of the areas which were brought under Russian rule had no strongly marked national traditions of their own to make them keenly resistant to assimilation; and a large part of the conquered territory was very sparsely populated and therefore easily open to Russian colonisation. The Russian agricultural system of peasant holdings was extended over a large part of the great plains; and the Russian colonist fitted in without much difficulty and readily accepted the hardships of settlement. There were frequent rebellions of the conquered peoples against the repressive autocracy of Russian rule; but they were, except in the case of Poland, mostly local, and either easily repressed or dealt with by incorporating the rebel groups as Cossacks under their own headmen in the military service of the Russian State. Russia had no colonial problems resembling those of the countries which built up their empires across the seas. It had neither colonies of its own people so separate geographically from the home country as to tend inevitably towards self-government nor far-off conquered territories climatically and economically unsuitable for white settlement. Nor was there, to any great extent, in the expansion of the Russian Empire, a process of " the flag following trade ". In the main " the flag " came first, and trade followed — but not much trade because of the predominantly agrarian character of Russia itself and of the narrow basis of Russian industry.

Indeed, until after 1870, industrial expansion played only a very small part in Russian imperialist policy. Thereafter, the building of the railways had a considerable effect, first in stimulating the development of a native iron industry — largely pioneered by an Englishman, John Hughes, at Ekaterinoslav — and, secondly, in promoting both internal trade between the complementary economic regions of forest, cornlands and grazing lands and also foreign trade — especially the large-scale export of corn. The growth of trade in turn led to a greater use of money, and the emancipated serfs gradually went over in part to a money economy based on selling their produce instead of living by subsistence farming. The pace of economic development and of import of foreign capital, mainly from France, increased rapidly towards the latter end of the nineteenth century, under the influence of Count Witte, and there was a further acceleration shortly before the First World War. But though the factories erected during these periods were mostly large and heavily equipped with up-to-date machinery, they constituted only a small sector of the total economy, and the industrial proletariat was only a small minority of the people. Moreover, there continued to be a great shortage of Russian technicians, and even of skilled workers in the mechanical industries. Up to the end of the nineteenth century the numbers employed in handicraft production, largely in artels and other types of co-operative production, exceeded the number of factory workers.

Factory labour in Russia developed, on the whole, under conditions considerably different from those of the West. Large-scale Russian industry had begun mainly in factories run either by the State or by large landowners with serf labour under conditions of extreme exploitation. As it became necessary to improve conditions in order to attract workers after the emancipation of the serfs, the improvements were made on paternalistic lines. The State and large private employers alike erected factories which, to a considerable extent, housed their employees and provided such amenities and services as were deemed to be necessary. There was no *laissez-faire* philosophy to stand in the way of paternalism or of State factory regulation; but there was a very strong resistance to allowing any form of working-class combination. Trade Unions were stamped out almost as soon as they arose, lest they should become points of focus for revolutionary agitation. The autocracy could not tolerate any attempt by the workers to organise for mutual self-help; and, accordingly, whatever was done to improve conditions in order to attract labour was done by legislation or by paternalistic action by the employing classes. Russian industry grew up under strict State tutelage; and the big industrial establishments in the mining and metal trades developed as company- or State-owned industrial villages, in which repression and paternalistic provision existed side by side This was less true of the textile industries, which were more scattered and usually on a smaller scale. But in metal-working and mining, and also later in the oil industry, industrialisation took shape in such a way as to create the very conditions of working-class solidarity it was designed to repress, and to prepare the way for the great paternalistic establishments developed by the Bolsheviks after the Revolution of 1917. Working-class organisation, driven underground, was handed over to revolutionary Socialist leadership. In the Revolution of 1905 the Soviets appeared spontaneously in the great industrial centres on the basis of the factory groups organised largely under Social Democratic influence.

The Revolution of 1905 was the immediate sequel to Russia's defeat in the war against Japan. The Trans-Siberian Railway, begun in 1891, had opened the way not only for increased settlement in Asiatic Russia but also for a further drive in the Far East. The Sino-Japanese War of 1894 provided a further opportunity. France and Russia, with Germany, intervened on China's side and compelled the Japanese to give up the Liaotung Peninsula. The Russians, with French help, gave China a large loan, and in return secured in 1896 a treaty which allowed them to build a railway, connecting with the Trans-Siberian line, across Manchuria to Vladivostok. Two years later the Russians occupied the Liaotung area, and in 1900 they marched into Manchuria. The Japanese, after long and fruitless negotiations, retaliated in 1904 by a sudden attack on the Russian fleet in Port Arthur, and in the ensuing struggle the Russians met with a severe defeat. The Treaty of Portsmouth (1905) involved the cession to Japan of half the island of Sakhalin and of the right to occupy Liaotung; and the Russians were also forced to evacuate Manchuria, where their place was speedily taken by the Japanese.

The Revolution of 1905 led to the granting of a Constitution and to the convocation of a Parliament — the Duma; but the new assembly was given only restricted powers. Dominated by the Cadets, the liberal party of the middle classes, which aimed at the establishment of a system of representative government on the Western model and at the speedier development of capitalist enterprise, the first Duma of 1906 at once fell foul of the Government, and was speedily dissolved. The same fate befell its successor the following year. The Government then restricted the franchise, and secured a more amenable assembly, which lasted from 1907 to 1912. From that date the Government became much more repressive, and political and industrial unrest developed apace. There were great strikes, violently suppressed, in St. Petersburg, Moscow, Baku and other areas in 1913 and 1914. At the outbreak of the First World War Russia appeared to be already on the verge of a second Revolution.

When war broke out in 1914 Russia had a number of large modern factories, equipped mainly with foreign machinery and carried on largely with the aid of foreign technical and managerial skill. The workers employed in them were in part life-long wage-earners; but they included many migrants from peasant homes who looked forward to returning to their villages after a period of factory work and could readily be attracted away from the factories by any prospect, such as arose on the morrow of the Revolution of 1917, of getting a share in the land. Russian industry was thus doubly vulnerable. Many of the technicians were Germans, and left the country on or before the outbreak of war; and both before and after the Revolution there was a loss of man-power, at first mainly to the armed forces and later on, with the breakdown of the Russian economy, as more and more workers streamed back to the villages in search of food and land. The transport system, quite inadequate to meet the demands of mobilisation on a vast scale added to normal economic demands, fell into chaos. The factories, unable to secure renewals of imported equipment or to get repairs executed, lapsed into grievous inefficiency. The arrangements for feeding the town populations broke down. The first Revolution of 1917 was mainly the outcome of intolerable strain and distress, made the greater by inefficiency and corruption at every level of the administrative machine. Russian industrial production had fallen catastrophically before the Revolution; and for some time afterwards it fell faster still as supplies of equipment from abroad were cut off and a large section of the industrial proletariat had to be taken away from the factories to fight in the civil war.

There is no room in this brief study to recount even in the barest outline the story of the gradual emergence of the Russian economy from the parlous state to which it had been reduced by the impact of war and revolution. The working force of industry had to be gradually recreated: the peasants had to be persuaded or coerced into supplying the towns with the means of life — a hard task because the towns had so little to offer them in return. The country passed, under Bolshevik rule, through the successive stages of "War Communism" and the "New Economic Policy". In the first of these stages the workers in most cases took over the running of the factories, from which most of the former managers and owners had fled or been expelled. There was no possibility of efficient running with much of the machinery worn out or broken and irreplaceable and with an acute shortage of skilled workers; but the extreme form of workers' control, establishment by establishment, exaggerated the chaos, and before long the Bolsheviks were engaged in a struggle to restore factory discipline and to reorganise the key industries under strongly centralised control, enforced by the strict discipline of the Communist Party, which was used to restore the authority of new, centrally appointed managers acting under political control. At the same time Lenin instituted the New Economic Policy, under which private trading by peasants and small-scale industrial producers was restored, while the Government kept a tight hand on the key industries and set to work to develop the heavy industries for the production of capital equipment and of arms for the Red Army. Lenin also launched the nation-wide plan of electrification, which involved entering into deals with foreign capitalists for the supply of equipment and of technical services; and concessions were granted to foreign concerns that were prepared to work in Russia on terms reminiscent of the methods of Czarism. These steps were taken, not because the Bolsheviks liked them, but in order to avoid absolute collapse. Lenin believed that, provided the Government kept a tight political hold over the country, it would be possible to prevent any real re-establishment of capitalist power, and to take back what had been conceded temporarily as soon as the immediate crisis had been overcome.

Lenin's electrification scheme met with much ridicule at the time when it was launched. It was regarded as absurdly ambitious because it was based on the assumption of an immense development in the demand for power. Most people believed that the new Communist society, faced with the urgent demand for more consumers' goods to raise the appallingly low standards of life, would find it impossible to set aside any appreciable part of its limited productive capacity for the making of capital goods. The peasants, it was argued, would starve the townsmen into submission if any attempt were made to expand industrial plant at the expense of the supply of consumers' goods. In practice, however, aided by the New Economic Policy, the Communist Government did gradually succeed both in getting the towns fed and in launching tremendously ambitious schemes of industrial development; and in these schemes, partly for military reasons and partly because the new rulers of Russia were determined at any cost to convert their country into a great modern industrial State, the first place was given to the heavy industries and the supplies of consumers' goods were increased only to a much smaller extent. The carrying through of this policy involved great ruthlessness, and there were sharp differences of opinion about its practicability among the Bolshevik leaders themselves; but under Stalin's leadership it was energetically pursued, and those who questioned it met with short shrift. The New Economic Policy was given up as soon as it had achieved its immediate purpose; and in 1928 the Soviet Union embarked on the first of its Five-Year Plans — the continuation and development of the electrification plan which Lenin had set out as the essential foundation for the new economy of the Socialist system.

Industrial development on the grand scale was, however, only one aspect of the comprehensive economic change which the new Bolshevik leadership was determined to bring about. The redistribution of the land, followed by the New Economic Policy, had involved a great development of peasant farming and had enabled many peasants to become substantial owners and profit-makers. These richer peasants, known as *kulaks*, were entrenched as leaders in much of the countryside and formed a powerful potential opposition to the Communist control of the society. As long as they retained their position, the Bolsheviks felt in serious danger and were aware of the impossibility of bringing the villages over to a Communist faith or way of life. Accordingly, Stalin decided, as soon as he felt strong enough, to embark on the policy of agricultural collectivisation. The peasants were to be forced to abandon their individual holdings and to pool their labour and resources in collective farms including whole village areas. In order to " get up steam " for this policy it was felt to be necessary to stir up the poorer peasants against the *kulaks*, who were ruthlessly persecuted and dispossessed, great numbers of them being removed from their holdings to timber camps and great constructional projects on which they were set to work under conditions of strict, almost convict, discipline and severe physical hardship. The lands of the *kulaks* were then thrown into the new collective farms, which were in effect compulsory co-operative societies designed to " socialise " the minds as well as the agricultural methods of their members.

This policy, pursued at breakneck speed and with a disregard for the immediate consequences, led to a vast slaughtering of livestock, which the peasants killed off rather than transfer them to collective ownership. It also led to much dislocation of arable production; and, coinciding with conditions of drought over large areas, was followed by widespread famine. Collectivisation had to be slowed down by direct orders from the Government; but the policy was not reversed. During the 1930s the collective system was introduced over most of the cultivated area of the Soviet Union, and at the same time the Communists continued with the policy, launched soon after the Revolution, of breaking up untilled land by mechanical cultivation through large State farms. These were at first very large indeed, and, being found unmanageable, were gradually divided into smaller, but still very considerable units. When collectivisation of the peasant holdings had been virtually completed there was some relaxation of the strict conditions which had been enforced in the earlier stages. Peasants were again given a limited right to own livestock individually and to undertake a certain amount of small-scale agricultural production as a supplement to their collective labours. But the great transformation was carried through with such completeness as virtually to eradicate the peasant system. One effect of the change was to make possible a greater use of machinery and the introduction of more modern agricultural methods; but the still very primitive state of knowledge among most of the villagers stood in the way of any rapid increase in productivity. The yield of Russian agriculture remained low, and the depleted livestock population was only slowly replenished. Still, under the successive Five-Year Plans there was a continuous increase in the output of agricultural machinery, especially tractors, and the great central tractor stations set up by the Government were used as means both of getting more modern practices adopted and of bringing into the countryside industrially minded tractor-operators to help in the process of "socialising" the minds of the people.

Meanwhile, under the stimulus given by a high rate of investment, industrial production was going up by leaps and bounds. There had always been too many peasants on the lands cultivated by primitive methods wasteful of man-power; and despite the continuous extension of the cultivated area, there were plenty of surplus workers who could be drawn from the countryside to supply labour for industry. The levels of productivity both on the land and in industry remained low by Western standards; but they rose a long way above those of the period of economic dislocation during and after the First World War, and were also, by the end of the 1920s, above the standards of the years before 1914. Agricultural output then suffered a severe temporary setback, while industrial production continued its rapid advance, especially in the heavy industries. Transport conditions also improved, not only on the railways, but also as great projects of canal-making were carried into effect. Russia's industrial advance continued almost unaffected by the world depression of the 1930s: it was proudly proclaimed that the Soviet Union was "the land without unemployment" and that Socialism had solved once and for all the problem of

PRODUCTION IN THE SOVIET UNION, 1929–39

	1929	1934	1938	1939
Wheat, million quintals	215 *	304	409	..
Cotton " "	2·2	3·6	8·8	8
Wool, thousand metric tons	179	58	137	136
Rayon " "	0·3	5·4	95	109
Cement, million metric tons	2·4	3·5	5·7	5·2
Petroleum " "	14	24	24	30
Coal " "	42	94	133	146
Iron Ore " "	8	10·8	13·5	14
Steel " "	5	9·7	18	18·8
Copper, thousand metric tons	26	44	84	107
Lead " "	6	27	69	75
Zinc " "	3	27	80	90
Bauxite (crude), thousand metric tons	12	61	250	270
Electricity, million kWh	6224	21,016	39,600	..
General Index of Industrial Production	100	260 †	413	482

* Average 1925–9 † 1935.

economic crises, which capitalism had shown itself powerless to prevent. By 1939, according to the Russian estimate, industrial production had risen 382 per cent above the level of 1929, and even the much less favourable estimate of the German Economic Institute put the increase at 244 per cent. The table on this page gives, from League of Nations sources, the estimates for a number of the principal commodities. The figures for wool, in sharp contrast to the others, reflect the great fall in the numbers of livestock which resulted from the enforcement of agricultural collectivisation. The numbers of cattle and sheep had not even by 1939 recovered to the levels which had been reached in 1930.

The rapid advance of production in the Soviet Union was sharply arrested in 1941 by the German attack. The German armies overran a large part of European Russia, and engaged in a deliberate course of slaughter and utter destruction. The Russians accomplished miracles in the evacuation of machinery, livestock, and stocks of goods, as well as of man-power, from the areas that were laid waste, and in the re-erection of evacuated plant and the resettlement of evacuated people in areas beyond the reach of the Nazis. The Western countries helped them with large supplies of war equipment, but could not do much towards rebuilding the shattered industries while the war lasted. Fortunately for the Russians, there had been during the 1930s a deliberate policy of developing industrial production in the Urals and in Asia and in siting new factories in Europe well away from the frontier. But the German advance penetrated so deeply into the south-eastern areas of European Russia that many of the great installations built in the inter-war period were destroyed. The destruction swept across the Ukraine and the Don and Donetz regions and reached the oil-fields of the Caucasus. It was arrested only at Moscow and at Stalingrad on the Volga — and, in the north, at Leningrad, which withstood years of siege. In 1945, when the Nazis at length collapsed, the Russians had to face a tremendous problem of industrial and agricultural reconstruction.

This task was tackled with ruthless energy. The fourth Five-Year Plan, running from 1946 to 1950, set a target for industry which required by the final year a level of output 48 per cent above that of 1940 — the last pre-war year. According to the official figures, the Plan was fulfilled in four years and a quarter, and the actual output of 1950 was 73 per cent above that of ten years before. In agriculture, the grain harvest of 1950 was 5½ million tons above that of 1940, and the yield 16 per cent higher. The cotton crop increased nearly threefold. The number of cattle on collective farms rose by 40 per cent, sheep and goats by 63 per cent, pigs by 49 per cent and poultry by 100 per cent. But the total number of livestock in the country was still only 4 per cent larger than in 1940, and that of poultry only 14 per cent.

Railway traffic showed an increase of 21 per cent over 1940, and inland water transport 26 per cent. Sea-borne cargoes rose by 65 per cent. Motor transport of goods was three times larger. Coal production was up by 57 per cent; oil by 22 per cent; electric power by 87 per cent. The output of machine tools was trebled, and there were even larger increases in electrical and power machinery. Agricultural machinery increased nearly fourfold. The output of chemicals was nearly trebled. Timber lagged behind, with a rise of only 36 per cent.

The consumers' goods industries mostly showed much smaller advances than the heavy industries. Clothing output, for example, rose by only 17 per cent above the level of 1940. But in these branches of production there had been a tremendous fall between 1940 and 1945. The supply of consumers' goods remained very short, even in 1950; but it was a great deal better than it had been during and immediately after the war. The Russians, however, under pressure of their fears, were still giving a high priority to the heavy industries, which provide the basis for war equipment as well as for general economic development.

Thus, in face of appalling difficulties and set-backs, Russia under its Communist rulers has undergone the swiftest economic transformation in human history. The Soviet Union has been endeavouring to leap straight from the most primitive methods of productive enterprise to the most advanced, skipping all the intermediate stages through which America and Western Europe have passed during the past two hundred years. Indeed, the Russians are attempting at one leap to advance in the mobilisation of economic resources much further than the United States or Great Britain or any other capitalist country has advanced even after two centuries of continuous development based on capitalistic enterprise. They are seeking to mobilise for the new industrialism the entire resources of a vast country extending over two continents and to develop all their massive projects as parts of a single comprehensive plan and under a completely unified control. In other industrial countries, even where considerable sectors have been nationalised and economic planning has become a recognised function of government, industrial production is still mainly a matter of private enterprise carried on by numerous independent profit-seeking concerns ; and in the United States, which has outrun all other countries in the scale and productivity of its industrial achievement, capitalism, far from perishing as a consequence of the inherent contradictions which caused Karl Marx to predict its speedy downfall a century ago, has passed through the ordeals of the great depression of the 1930s without the collapse which then seemed to be threatening it, and has become the protagonist in a world crusade against the " Communist menace " to the capitalist way of life.

The Soviet peoples, under the inspiration of Nikolai Lenin, made up their minds to leap straight from a primitive peasant civilisation into the age of electricity and giant power. They set out under their Communist rulers to accomplish in a few years all and more than all that Western capitalism had accomplished in two centuries of gradual development. It was possible for the Russians to undertake so colossal a task, not only because they had great resources and abundant man-power, but also because it is characteristic of modern mechanical development to proceed at an ever-increasing pace. When power-driven machinery was first introduced its advance was, by any modern standard, slow and hesitant. Watt's steam-engine, on which the material progress of the nineteenth century was largely based, achieved no speedy triumph. Even in Great Britain its use spread but slowly for a long time, and fifty years after its introduction there were still a great many industries and processes which it had invaded hardly at all. In other countries its progress was slower still. It did not conquer the greater part of the textile industry of either France or Germany until well after the middle of the nineteenth century; and in every industry and country it made its way piecemeal and by painful stages in face of the strong resistance of employers as well as workers to the abandonment of traditional crafts and methods of production.

Nevertheless, as the nineteenth century advanced, the pace of mechanical change grew much more rapid; for when the transition to a productive system based on mechanical power had once been made, the improvement of machines and the devising of new methods of production were bound to proceed at an increasing speed. One invention leads to another; and manufacturers, eager to reduce their costs of production, had to be constantly on the look-out for new devices, unless they were able to establish themselves in a position of monopoly which allowed them to make profits without keeping their methods up to date. Moreover, as the workers became organised and able to insist on higher wages and better conditions of employment, even the monopolist was usually driven to seek new ways of getting good value for his money by making the dearer labour more productive or reducing the quantity of it which he used by finding machines to do work previously done by men's physical strength. Competition between employers and between countries to cut down costs and the desire to reduce prices in order to sell more goods led to a growingly rapid advance in mechanisation; for it was soon discovered that for many kinds of goods great economies could be achieved by producing on a larger scale, as well as by combining to control the market. The scale of production grew larger, and the scale of business enterprise larger still. Capital was aggregated into greater masses, and the new means which were devised in order to promote the aggregation of capital — through the development of the joint-stock system — made possible the provision of more and more extensive assemblages of plant and machinery. Mechanisation moved on faster and faster towards a goal that came to appear to be nothing less than the complete elimination of man's physical strength as a factor in the productive process.

The Soviet Union, in its whole-hearted enthusiasm for the ideal of a mechanical way of life, has accomplished prodigies; but, in comparison with the United States, its principal rival in this as in other matters, its productivity is still very low. In agriculture, its yields are low even on the very favourable soils of the black belt — whether yield per acre or yield per worker be taken as the standard. In industry, too, the output of the average worker is a long way below West European as well as American levels, despite the much publicised achievements of Stakhanovites and the adoption of systems of incentive payment which offer strong inducements to effort. Productivity in both agriculture and industry is rising; but it has a long way to go before it can catch up with the countries where industrialisation has been accepted for more than a century. Moreover, in terms of the whole standard of living, the exceedingly overcrowded housing conditions, which little has been done to remedy, have to be set against the improvements in the supply of consumers' goods; and even these have increased much less than the rise in total output would suggest, both because priority has been given to the heavy industries and because of the very rapid rate at which population has increased.

The Soviet Union has to-day a swiftly rising population, in which the younger age-groups constitute an exceptionally high proportion of the whole. The inhabitants of the Soviet Union now number upwards of 200 millions; and there is every probability of the rapid rate of increase continuing, in view of falling infant mortality and a rising expectation of life for those who survive infancy. This of course means that a large annual increase in production is needed to keep the standard of living constant. Moreover, as the development of industry involves large-scale migration from the countryside to the towns, old and new, a great deal of new construction is needed to keep pace with the needs of the town-dwellers, not only for houses, but for all kinds of public services. As we saw, housing has, despite these conditions, hitherto been given only a low priority, in comparison with industrial development and even with public amenities. The Russian workers are used to hard living; but it seems clear that before long it will become absolutely necessary to devote a larger proportion of productive resources to improving conditions of living in the urban areas.

This small book is not the place for a discussion of the "cold war", which, since the announcement of the Marshall Plan and the "Truman Doctrine", has divided most of the world into two great centres of rearmament and mutual suspicion. It is relevant here only to point out that in the West present-day Russian policy is widely interpreted by Governments as essentially a continuation of the Czarist policies of the past. Russia, it is argued, has been for centuries an expansionist military Power bent on the extension of its control all round the long land frontiers which are the outcome of past conquests.

Historically, the Russians have been, over a long period, driving westward over Europe, eastward towards and down the coast lands of the Far East, south-eastward into the Near and Middle East, and southward from their Asiatic territories into and beyond Central Asia. The emphasis, and the success of the various drives, have differed from time to time; and there have been serious reverses — for example in the Far East in 1905, in Europe after the First World War, and in northern Persia after 1945. But the will to expansion has been continuous, though nowadays it appears to be taking a different form and to be directed not to annexation but to the establishment of Communist Governments ready to follow the Russian lead. Poland, Hungary, Roumania and Bulgaria are Soviet satellites, as Yugoslavia too was up to the break between Marshal Tito and the Russians in 1948. Finland, though not a satellite, has to conform to Russian demands in matters affecting foreign policy. China, aided by the handing over of Manchuria, with its considerable industrial resources and equipment, has become a Communist State and, in face of America's continued support of Chiang Kai-shek in Formosa, cannot afford to quarrel with the Soviet Union. The Chinese have occupied Tibet and have gone to the assistance of the Government set up by the Soviet Union during its occupation of North Korea. Communists dominate the Viet-Minh Government in Indo-China, against which the French are fighting what seems likely to be an interminable war. The civil war in Malaya is sustained mainly by Chinese Communists. In Persia, though the Soviet Union has been careful since the set-backs of a few years ago to avoid open intervention, Communist supporters have done their utmost to fan nationalist sentiment against British imperialism as represented by the British-owned Anglo-Iranian Oil Company. In all the Arab States and in every colonial territory they can reach, the Communists support anti-imperialist movements. In Greece their supporters have been defeated mainly by American and British aid to a succession of weak Governments. The Communists have also met with defeat in Indonesia and Burma, and have failed to establish their position in India and Pakistan. But, as against this, they have built up powerful support in the West among the working classes of Italy, still direly poor, and of France, where, despite economic recovery, working-class standards of living have been falling because of the failure to control prices or to use taxation efficiently as an instrument for redistributing wealth.

It is extraordinarily difficult to say how far the policies of the Soviet Union since 1945 are to be regarded as the expression of a continued Russian expansionism resting on nationalistic foundations, and how far as logical applications of the theory of Marxism. According to Marxian theory, capitalism is destined to be superseded all over the world by a form of Socialism resting on the dictatorship of the proletariat. It is the " historic mission " of the proletariat to make an end of capitalist and imperialist exploitation and to establish the " classless society ". The Russian leaders, as Marxists, regard this outcome as inevitable, and as doubtful only in the manner and time of its coming. They also regard it as inevitable that the world's capitalists, now represented chiefly by the United States, should attempt to destroy the Communist system of government in the Soviet Union and elsewhere as a threat to their own survival. Recent Soviet policy is intelligible in the light of these dogmas, as based partly on fear of the Americans and partly on a consistent desire to aid the cause of world revolution in all countries not already under Communist control. On this view of the matter, it is not necessary to invoke the explanation of Russian policy as essentially a continuation of the imperialist expansionism of the past. But it seems reasonable to suggest that in the minds of the present rulers of the Soviet Union the two elements are inextricably mingled. This is strongly indicated by the marked tendency in recent years to claim as Russian inventions more and more of the great discoveries which lie at the foundations of modern industrialism, as well as to dwell on the achievements of Czarist Russia, which used to be so fervently denounced.

On the other hand, it is impossible to dismiss the Russian fears of America as groundless. The policy of the United States Government is officially described as "containment" — that is, as aiming not at destroying Communism in the Soviet Union but at resisting in force every attempt by the Communists to expand the area under their control. In the case of China, it goes further by refusing to accept the accomplished fact of Communist control of the country. This policy in itself is calculated, in the Far East, where it has involved not only support for Chiang Kai-shek but also the conversion of Japan into an American military base, to keep up indefinitely a state of tension that may easily at any time lead to large-scale war; but there are also exceedingly vocal sections of American opinion which openly preach the need for a more aggressive policy and treat war with the Soviet Union as virtually inevitable. When, early in 1951, President Truman dismissed General MacArthur from his position as virtual ruler of Japan, the effect was not so much a repudiation of the General's policy as a partial acceptance of it in order to consolidate support behind the Government.

The reader, however, must decide for himself how far to regard the Soviet Union, from the standpoint of world politics, as the heir to Czardom, and how much stress to lay on the Marxian doctrine of world revolution as the explanation of current Soviet policies. In this book the main concern is with the economic factors. Unless world war is renewed — with consequences of which it would be futile to attempt any prediction — the Soviet Union is clearly destined to make, during the coming decades, immense strides in productivity and to come much nearer to the standards of Western Europe, if not to those of the United States. This factor alone is enough to alter the economic shape of the world to a prodigious extent; for the peoples that remain sunk in primary poverty cannot help being more and more affected in their attitudes by the transformation of the Soviet Union into a great industrial country with an economic system basically different from capitalism. Even if the Russians were entirely unaggressive and wholly prepared to co-operate pacifically with the capitalist parts of the world, without any attempt to stir up troubles or revolution, the very existence of a vast non-capitalist area equipped with the most modern economic techniques would constitute a constant challenge, which could be successfully met only if means could be found for starting the economically backward countries on a course of development that would hold out real promise of a rapidly improving standard of life. On this great question there will be more to say in the following chapter.

XI

Machines and Men

THE changes described in this book have rested on a foundation of technical and scientific discovery. It is necessary to use both adjectives because many of the key inventions and improvements, at any rate during the earlier part of the period here studied, owed nothing to professional scientists, or even to learned men. They were made and added to by men who had only the training of practical experience, and sometimes not even that. Cartwright, who made the first power-loom and also a pioneer wool-combing machine, was a clergyman who wrote verses; Hargreaves, who invented the spinning jenny, and Crompton, who invented the " mule ", were both textile operatives; John Kay, who introduced the flying shuttle, was a small employer; Arkwright started as a barber. Benjamin Huntsman, who first made cast steel, was a clockmaker. These are only a few out of many examples: even James Watt and George Stephenson were craftsmen rather than scientifically trained technicians.

This is not at all surprising; for the eighteenth century, despite its intense interest in the practical arts, offered few opportunities for scientific or technical training except through apprenticeship; and many of the most important inventions, especially in the textile trades, were the products of common sense and ingenuity rather than of applied scientific knowledge. As long as it was mainly a question of devising or improving machine-tools to take over some manual process or to produce a product of better quality, the attainments needed in the inventor were such as an ingenious man could fairly easily acquire either in an old-established manual craft, such as clockmaking, or as an amateur — or perhaps as an innovating landowner or farmer with a taste for mechanical experiment. In agriculture, too, the new methods that made the greatest practical difference were arrived at rather by practical experiments carried on in the spirit of trial and error than by the use of strictly scientific techniques. This was as true of Bakewell's improvements in stock-breeding as of the Norfolk plough.

The age of the Industrial Revolution began mainly as a period of discoveries in the realm of practical mechanics. Chemistry played only a small part in its earlier phases, and biology, save of the most rough and ready sort, none at all. Electricity remained a toy, and even metallurgy was mainly in the hands of practical producers rather than of scientists. The character of industrial development changed as the emphasis shifted from the making of machines for the direct replacement of hand processes to the provision of power-plant for driving them; for in this field difficult scientific problems necessarily presented themselves — problems of metallurgy which could be solved only by experts, problems of fuel economy and utilisation of waste energy, problems of deep mining and of other dangerous trades, problems of weight and stress and tension which demanded laboratory work. Of course, such problems had in many cases existed earlier — for example, in bridge-building and in other branches of civil engineering. But they had been much less central.

As the chemical aspects of industry grew in importance, and as electricity came to be seriously considered as a source of power, the processes of production came to rest much more widely on a foundation of scientific techniques. A quite sharp difference appeared between the industries which were based mainly on the growing achievements of the physical sciences and those which were not, as far as their manufacturing operations were concerned. Metallurgy, chemical production and electrical engineering formed the core of the former group, with other branches of engineering more or less closely related to them: textiles, clothing and most of the other industries supplying consumers' goods still belonged to the second group, even when they used complicated power-driven machinery devised and supplied by the engineers. Mining held an intermediate position, with a tendency to depend more on scientifically trained engineers and chemists as mine-shafts were driven deeper and as the extraction of by-products became a growingly important source of profit. Of course, the advance of labour-saving machine tools continued side by side with these developments; but for a long period, extending over most of the second half of the nineteenth century, its effects were much less spectacular than they had been at the time of the great discoveries in the textile trades. The engineering industry, aided by Whitworth's precision gauges and by successive improvements in the centre lathe and the development of many specialised machines based upon it, and also by power-forging and greater variety and standardisation of the metals on which it worked, provided, for a wide range of industries, machines which made less exacting calls on the personal skill of the machine-operator, at any rate when no high degree of fine adjustment was required. But these changes came gradually and were accompanied by so great an expansion of demand that they seldom displaced large masses of skilled workers, as the power-loom had done in the textile trades. Indeed, in most cases the demand for skilled workers increased rapidly, and the problem, except in periods of depression, was rather to find enough of them than to turn them away as no longer needed.

A new phase set in early in the present century, at first mainly in the United States, where mass-immigration was providing a very large supply of unskilled workers and there was a rapidly expanding market for consumers' goods. These conditions led to the development of new techniques of mass-production, based largely on machines designed not only for the execution of long runs of uniform specialised processing, but also for the elimination as far as possible of normal skill as distinct from mere dexterity. The workers on these new machines were required to work fast; but as far as possible the machines were made "fool-proof" and automatic, in order to allow of a hot pace without spoiling the work. On this revolutionary development of mechanisation was soon superimposed a further change, as the automatisation of the work-process began to be consciously applied to the workers themselves, as well as to the machines. F. W. Taylor coined the phrase "Scientific Management" to describe the new approach: time-study and motion-study, aimed at discovering how quickly a process could be carried through and what motions the operators should make in order to carry it through as quickly as possible, came into fashion. These developments were speedily followed by the advent of the moving platform and the assembly line: the Ford car was the first outstanding achievement of the new technique.

These methods of automatisation could not, of course, be applied universally. They required a very large market for a standardised product, the making of which could be broken up largely into a succession of fool-proof processes. But it appeared before long that the range of their application could be very wide, not only in the metal-working trades but also for a great variety of consumers' goods and in packaging as well as in actual manufacture. The economy of standardised mass-production in these fields was very great. At first, a part of the attraction had been, as in the textile trades in the Industrial Revolution, the possibility of using cheap, unskilled labour; but it was soon found, when the mass-supply of immigrants to the United States was cut off after 1914, that high mechanisation so reduced wage-cost as a proportion of total cost as to make this factor relatively unimportant. The rise of wages in the United States did not check the process: it hastened development, by providing a further incentive to substitute machines for men and to extract from the human factor of production the full economic benefits of highly standardised work.

The first half of the twentieth century was also marked by a great advance in the development of raw materials, chemically produced — rayon and staple fibre, the wide variety of "plastics", synthetic rubber and synthetic oil. These changes increased the dependence of industry on science and brought the chemists right into the centre of the industrial arts. At the same time the cost of experimentation and research, over the whole field of industry, rose sharply. Only very big firms, with enormous markets, could afford to develop the research laboratories that were coming to be indispensable if methods were to be kept up to date. The individual inventor, the man with an idea, found himself in more and more instances quite unable to proceed unless he could get a big concern to back him and provide him with a staff and equipment. Moreover, even when a new process had been fully tested out in the laboratory, there was often a still more costly stage ahead before it could be applied; for there were problems of plant construction and right adaptation of processes which could be solved only by "development" of research on a full commercial scale. To some extent, smaller firms which could not afford to carry on their own research were helped by the establishment of State-aided Research Associations open to entire industries; but it was found that in many cases the smaller firms had not staffs capable of understanding or applying the information and advice which the Associations put at their disposal.

Thus the gap widened both between the few fully equipped firms and the general run of smaller firms in the industries in which methods of mass-production were being applied, and also between these industries and those which rested less on foundations of highly technical scientific knowledge. There was also a widening of the gap between average productivity in the United States and in Europe, not because the average American workman was more skilled or worked harder — his working hours were fewer — nor because American scientists were cleverer than Europeans, but rather because of the immense size of the American market and of the much greater expenditure on research and development in the United States. The Soviet Union, still far behind, is now copying the American techniques at a furious pace; the countries of Western Europe are being adjured to copy them, but are lagging behind, mainly for two reasons. The first reason is that the assured markets of these countries are much smaller, so that the full development of standardisation would be possible only if there were some agreed pooling of markets among them, on the basis of a common production plan that would encourage national specialisation. The second reason is that the capital required for any comprehensive re-equipment of West European industry could be provided only at the expense of the immediate standards of living of the peoples; and the Western Governments are by no means in a position to impose low standards of living now in the interests of future wealth, as the Russians have been doing under their successive Five-Year Plans.

It has been left unquestioned, so far, in this chapter, that increased productivity is to be welcomed, without regard to its effects on the human factor in production —

that is, on man as a producer. Man as a consumer obviously wants more goods : even in the richest countries there are still a great many poor people who are going short. This may seem to constitute a sufficient case for welcoming the advances in mass-production ; but before we finally accept this view, we had better look rather more closely at the nature of the changes in human working conditions which mechanisation involves.

In this swiftly advancing mechanisation of industry there have been three distinct, though closely related, ways in which human labour has been transformed and replaced by the development of mechanical power.

In the first place, the limits set to productive capacity by the physical strength of the individual have been almost completely transcended. The weight that a machine can lift or the pressure that it can apply bears no relation at all to the physical strength, individual or collective, of those who manipulate its levers. A modern drop-hammer or mechanical crane is not merely a substitute for human energy : it is an individual force which no amount of such energy — not even the massed human strength that built the Pyramids — could supply. As technique improves, this new force can be applied on an ever-increasing scale. It is the very foundation on which modern methods of production in the heavy constructional industries have been built up.

Secondly, the machine serves as a substitute for the skill and acquired dexterity of the human worker. It carries out automatically and with a constantly improving accuracy countless jobs which had previously to be done by hand by repetition workers whom only long practice could make perfect. By the development of " fool-proof " machines the required period of training for work of this type is immensely shortened, and unskilled labour becomes much more readily interchangeable between one mechanical task and another. At the same time, as machines grow more delicate and complicated, they can be used more and more to replace not merely human dexterity but also the superior and more painfully acquired skill of the trained craftsman. In the making of machines, improvements in the processes of casting iron have eliminated a large part of the old skill, not only of moulders in sand and pattern-makers in wood, but also of fitters and turners in the later processes of machining and adjustment. Skilled labour does not cease to be needed — indeed in some branches of engineering work, such as toolmaking and the repairing of machinery, there is often a call for even higher skill than before. But for most forms of mechanised industry the proportion of highly skilled work to the total volume of employment is greatly and swiftly diminished. Nor is the machine content to stop short at the processes of production. It invades the office and the counting-house as well. The typewriter and the calculating machine have revolutionised the work of clerical and administrative departments of modern business ; and even the private home — the last province of the old manual drudgery — is being gradually revolutionised as the supply of domestic servants runs short — though in this case there is a long lag between the introduction of labour-saving devices and their availability to the main body of the people.

It is true, on the other hand, that the new machines have often called into being new types of skill and have sometimes resulted in replacing unskilled by skilled labour. The coming of modern mechanical engineering destroyed the traditional craft of the millwrights who made the old machines out of wood ; but it created the new skilled crafts of turning, fitting, drop-hammer forging and a host of others. Again, the coming of the factory system in the spinning of textile yarn replaced the " domestic " workers of the old hand-spinning processes by the highly skilled mule-spinners of the nineteenth century. But in more modern times mule spinning has been giving place to the much less skilled process of ring spinning; and the skilled work of fitters and turners is being more and more taken over by standardised casting and forging and by automatic and semi-automatic machine processes. The nineteenth century, to a great extent, created new skilled crafts in place of those which it destroyed. The twentieth century is going much further towards the transference of skill from the worker to the machine, and is thus reducing the proportion of skilled to less skilled workers, though it makes at the same time higher demands on the technicians and craftsmen who are still needed to make and to maintain and regulate the machines.

Thirdly, modern machinery not only dispenses more and more with the need for either physical strength or manual skill, but also goes further and further towards the positive displacement of labour. If a machine can be made as skilful as a man and as powerful as the combined labour of many men, the number of workers required for putting a given quantity of energy in motion can be reduced to a mere fraction of what it used to be. Anyone who visits, for example, a modern flour-mill will see how far this sheer elimination of labour can be pushed in an industry readily amenable to mechanisation.

Bring the grain alongside the wharf in the ship that has carried it from overseas. Stick a long pipe equipped with powerful suction into the ship's hold and with it suck the grain up to the top storey of the mill. Have the mill filled with automatic machines which separate, grind, sort and grade the grain, which is turned into flour as it descends automatically from floor to floor, until it is packed automatically into sacks and dropped automatically into lorries which will carry it away to wherever it is wanted. In all this sequence of processes no human hand need touch the grain, or even the machines that are at work upon it. There is no labour left at all save that of a few crane men, a few mechanics to oil the machines and keep them in order, and a worker or two with brooms and swabs, looking strangely out of place, to keep the mill swept and garnished. This is an extreme instance; but it is the end towards which all mass-production industry seems to be moving by an irresistible momentum. To replace and amplify man's physical strength, to replace and improve upon man's manual skill — these are not enough. The end of industrialism is to make the worker a merely incidental and rarer and rarer attendant upon the machine.

In the latest developments of industrialism the emphasis has been more and more upon this absolute displacement of labour. Indeed the stronger working-class organisation and the working-class demand for higher wages and better conditions become, the greater grows the pressure upon the employer to dispense with labour and to use machinery instead. While unskilled labour was cheap emphasis was laid largely on enabling unskilled men and women to do skilled men's work. So it still is in relatively backward countries; but in America and in Western Europe industrialism has passed beyond that stage. There are no longer any dirt-cheap reserves of workers to be exploited; and both skill and wages are relatively high. In these circumstances, the obvious way of lowering costs is to use less labour and more machine-power; and especially in America this form of rationalisation has been pushed to astonishing lengths.

Of course nothing but good ought to result from the tremendous increase in productive power which is the correlative of this economy in the use of labour. It ought to make possible at once a great advance in material standards of living and a lessening of the duration and intensity of work. But actually its effects were seen between the wars mainly in growing unemployment in the capitalist countries. Production did not expand in correspondence with the development of productive power; and the workers who were thrust out of their jobs were neither reabsorbed through the expansion of their old industries nor able to find sufficient openings elsewhere. Capitalist America and capitalist Britain alike experienced a contraction in the demand for labour side by side with the growing mechanisation of industry. A new term — "technological unemployment" — had to be coined in order to describe what was coming about.

This displacement of labour was the culmination of a process that had been at work ever since the first onset of the new mechanical power. It happened in the Industrial Revolution and it went on happening at a more and more rapid rate; but whereas in the earlier stages of industrialism the new openings for employment sufficed, though not without much transitional suffering, to reabsorb those who were displaced and to absorb the increasing populations of the capitalist countries, in the period between the wars it seemed as if the pace of expansion had so slowed down as to create a permanent surplus of workers for whom no jobs could be found. In the nineteenth century the countries which led the way in industrial development found rapidly growing markets open to them in the less developed regions of the world; but in the twentieth century it began to seem as if there were too many competitors equipped with the latest instruments of production and too few markets to which they could send their goods. Export — the nineteenth century's safety valve against unemployment — met with more and more obstacles as fresh countries set out to supply their own home markets and entered as rivals into the markets of the world. The total volume of world exports did not indeed grow less; but it was no longer expanding at the same rate as the productive capacity of capitalist industry.

In the meantime agriculture, which had owed its greatly increasing productivity during the nineteenth century fully as much to the exploitation of virgin soil as to improvements in its methods of cultivation, was also passing, in the advanced countries, through a revolution which carried with it a great economy in the use of labour power. The changes in agriculture have been in fact no less far-reaching than the changes in industry, though they have taken to some extent a different form. The agricultural revolution in Great Britain in the eighteenth and early nineteenth centuries had gone fully as deep as the revolution in industry and had advanced by even more rapid stages. Enclosures of the old common fields and of open lands, accompanied by improved methods of land drainage and husbandry, more scientific rotation of crops, and better facilities for marketing, had enormously increased the productivity of arable land. At the same time, more skilful breeding of sheep and cattle, the provision of winter feeding-stuffs made possible by enclosures, the development of root crops, and the growth of urban markets for meat, hides and wool, rendered profitable a huge advance in the intensity of agricultural enterprise.

This revolution in agriculture had been accompanied by a great displacement of labour from the rural areas; as long as land was enclosed mainly for the extension of arable cultivation, this was not because the new methods of tillage needed less labour than the old. It arose rather from two other causes. The first was that the old village system had maintained a host of people who got a bare living, not by systematically tilling the land, but by keeping a beast or a few geese on the common, raising perhaps a very small quantity of produce on a tiny patch of land, and hiring themselves out intermittently to farmers and for work on the roads. Enclosure drove these squatters and cottagers in large numbers from their tiny holdings, left them without status or means of livelihood in the villages, and thus forced them to migrate to the towns in search of work. Moreover, many of these villagers had eked out their incomes by the industrial by-employment of the women and children in occupations such as spinning. The second cause of rural depopulation was the passing of such trades from the cottages into the factory towns. These two causes were continuously at work in England during the agrarian revolution; and to them, after the Napoleonic wars, was added a third when the cessation of the abnormal war-time demand for wheat with the reopening of Continental markets caused a decrease in the cultivated area, and thus drove yet more villagers to seek their living in the towns. But this cause came later than the others, which were mainly responsible for the great rural exodus.

Thereafter the British farmer went on improving his methods of cultivation; and Continental agriculture, a long way behind the British in farming efficiency, advanced more slowly, mainly under a system of peasant holdings. In France the Revolution had given the peasants secure possession of the land, while in Germany the reforms of Stein and Hardenberg had begun the abolition of serfdom, and in East Prussia agricultural techniques made rapid progress on the great *junker* estates which were consolidated after the personal emancipation of the serfs.

As the century advanced, however, the conditions of world agriculture were revolutionised by the opening up of the New World. The new phase was marked at first not so much by improved methods of cultivation or stock-breeding as by the changed conditions for the transport of agricultural produce. Railroads opened up the interior of great continents in America and Australasia, and steamships brought the new supplies of grain and other produce more and more cheaply and in rapidly increasing quantities to the Old World from the New. Wheat came first;

but from the 'eighties, with the introduction of the refrigerator ship, the ranches of America and Australasia were able to supply the Old World with a growing proportion of its meat as well. Great Britain, as the richest country, with the best and cheapest manufactures to offer in exchange for food, became the principal market for the agriculture of the New World, and under the Free Trade system British agriculture gradually contracted and a new movement of rural depopulation set in, finding its outlets in emigration to the New World as well as in migration to the industrial areas. In terms of product per acre the new prairie lands could not compare with the more intensively farmed agricultural lands of Western Europe; but in cheapness the virgin soils of the New World had the advantage. Low farming with little labour paid best where men were few and land was plentiful and cheap.

The conditions of agriculture in the new countries thus gave an impetus to mechanisation. The farm tractor, the mechanical reaper-binder, and the other power-driven instruments of modern large-scale agriculture became the characteristic tools of the prairie farmer. Farming in the new areas also gave a stimulus to scientific advance in the selection of varieties of grain and stock that would thrive under various climatic conditions and in the fight against insect pests and diseases of plants and animals. Scientific research greatly increased the yield of cultivation, improved the weight and quality of stock, and enabled goods to be transported over long distances with less and less deterioration. It improved the quality and yield of wool, devised uses for waste products such as offals, and guided agriculture in supplying the needs of industry for new varieties of produce. Again and again it was prophesied that agricultural prices were bound to rise in relation to the prices of industrial goods because agriculture could not possibly emulate the mass-production methods of modern industry. But this did not happen: indeed, on the whole, the tendency was the other way. Over the past two centuries the revolution in agriculture, except in the backward countries, has fallen no whit short of the revolution in industry. The "law of diminishing returns" — that constant terror of the economists and politicians of the early nineteenth century — came to seem further and further off as new lands were opened up and productivity per man increased. The world came to complain, not of a shortage but of a glut of agricultural goods, despite the survival over a large part of its surface of peasant cultivation at a very low standard of efficiency. Not that the world ought to have been in any fear of a glut of food; for there were — and are still — among its inhabitants hundreds of millions with much too little to eat.

The new agricultural methods tended, however, equally with the new methods in industry, to the displacement of human labour in the raising of staple crops. But this tendency was to some extent offset by the growth of specialist forms of agriculture, such as the raising of market-garden and dairy produce, fruit, eggs and poultry, and also pigs, by more intensive methods for the supply of the growing urban populations—especially of the better-off. The developments of these types of agriculture, so successfully pursued in Denmark and Holland, depended on a continued rise in standards of living; for the products of specialist agriculture are for the most part consumed by those whose incomes provide for a surplus over the sheer necessities of living. The growth of specialist agriculture depends on the general level of prosperity in the communities to which its products are supplied. The maintenance of population in the rural areas of the advanced countries thus came to depend on the continued advance of industry, and a fall in industrial employment involved a contraction of rural employment as well. In the twentieth century, particularly after 1945, this tendency was modified by the appearance of "balance of payments" problems which forced a number of countries, including Great Britain, to grow a larger proportion of their own food, instead of importing it from abroad; but this involved production at high cost of foodstuffs which could have been imported with advantage if the means of payment had been available.

Taking the past two centuries as a whole, economic advance has consisted above all in the steady decrease in the amount of labour needed to produce and deliver into the hands of the consumers a given quantity of goods. This tendency alone has made possible the great rise in standards of living in every country which has adopted the new methods of production. Throughout the century between the Napoleonic Wars and the Great War of 1914, though there were from time to time serious frictions in the transference of labour from old to new types of employment, the international division of labour undoubtedly worked out to the great advantage of the more industrialised countries. The rapidly expanding world market enabled the advanced countries to increase their production for export, and to stimulate foreign demand by the export of capital to the less developed areas. But between the wars the export of capital suffered a check, and world demand failed to keep pace with the expansion of productive capacity, whereas the displacement of labour through mechanisation was proceeding faster than ever. There arose an apparent deficiency of consuming power in relation to the capacity of the productive system; and the world's most pressing problem seemed to be, not a further increase of the power to produce but the devising of means for the full use of the productive resources already at hand. This problem became the more serious because the advanced countries, in their endeavours to find an outlet for their surplus goods, attempted to expand their exports by cutting down their costs of production at the workers' expense and thus further decreased consumption in their home markets. The more this was done, the more unemployment increased, openly in the industrial areas and in the form of "concealed unemployment" in the peasant countries, where redundant labour was crowded upon the land to no productive purpose.

Until this manifestly absurd situation had continued for a considerable time, both Governments and capitalists in the advanced countries persisted in regarding it as incurable, and in denying that the level of employment in a country was a matter over which public policy could exert any substantial influence. The economic disasters of 1931 were needed to induce any change in this belief. Then at length the spread of unemployment in the United States forced that highly individualistic society into the work-finding policies of the "New Deal", and in Great Britain the writings of J. M. Keynes brought about a long-overdue revolution in economic thought. The maintenance of "full employment" came to be widely regarded not only as a desirable but also as an eminently practicable objective of public financial and economic policy; and the doctrine of the "right to work", hitherto proclaimed only by the Socialists, acquired respectability in the more advanced academic and business circles. Whereas the Socialists had argued that unemployment was a necessary disease of capitalism, Keynes and other protagonists of the "New Economics" held that full employment could be maintained under capitalism, provided that budgetary and banking policies were directed to that end and that the Government stood ready, by one means or another, to maintain the total of investment, private and public together, at the level needed to absorb the available supplies of labour.

The effect of this doctrine was to stake out a powerful claim in support, not of Socialism, but of a new type of planned capitalist economy involving a considerable measure of public control. It encountered, however, strong resistance from those who regarded such control as inconsistent with the requirements of " free enterprise "; and, under the conditions which existed after the Second World War, the opponents of the " New Economics " were able to rally their forces the better because in both Great Britain and the United States the problem of unemployment had ceased for the time being to exist in a serious form. In Great Britain, this disappearance was mainly due to the co-existence of an absolute necessity to produce as much as possible in order to maintain the standard of life and of a world-wide famine of industrial goods caused by the dislocations and devastations of the war years. In the United States it was due much more to the improved organisation and bargaining power of labour which had been brought about first by the New Deal and subsequently by the immense demands on American production during the years of war. American consuming power had increased almost step by step with productivity; and the demand for American goods was further reinforced after 1945 by the loans and gifts which were poured out in order to assist European recovery and to build up the " defence of the West " against the rising power of the Soviet Union. The Soviet economists continued to predict that these conditions of capitalist prosperity could not last, and that before long economic crisis would reappear in an aggravated form. But up to 1951 this had not happened: on the contrary, intensified spending on armaments was putting an ever-increasing strain on the man-power and resources of the leading capitalist countries.

Unemployment, however, had not, after 1945, been banished at all completely even from the capitalist world.

It remained very severe in Italy, which combined with an inconveniently rapid rate of increase in population, the disadvantages of an incredibly feudal and inefficient land system and a great shortage both of natural resources and of capital for economic development. Western Germany, with its host of displaced persons from the East, was a second sufferer; and Belgium and Denmark also had sizable problems of redundant labour. In general, however, the advanced capitalist countries of Europe had so much to do after the Second World War in rebuilding their economies as to be more conscious of shortage than of redundancy of workers; while in the United States the capitalist inhibitions of the 1930s seemed for the time being to have been overcome and, with the special stimuli of Marshall Aid to Europe and subsequently of intensive rearmament, there was in 1951 no shortage of jobs.

Were these jobs good enough — not so much in terms of pay as of their human quality? An ever-increasing proportion of them involved sheer routine work, done at a great pace, in huge establishments in which most of the workers were personally unknown one to another. At the end of the day's work many of them travelled long distances back to their homes under crowded and uncomfortable conditions. The employers of these workers in the mass-production industries were huge corporations, owned largely by shareholders who neither knew nor cared what was done with their money, provided that the profit was good. The real employers were in many cases salaried managers, who might or might not have an ownership share in the businesses they managed. Of recent years, Trade Unions probably negotiated the terms of employment; and there might or might not be consultative machinery of some sort in the factories. The thing that mattered most to most of the workers was the size of the pay-packet, with the nature of the work and the conditions under which it had to be done as secondary, though not unimportant, factors. A minority of highly skilled workers employed in maintenance work, tool-making, setting up machines, and other exceptional jobs might be able to take some pleasure in their work, or unconsciously get from it a sense of personal creative achievement. For the great majority there could be no such experience, unless it were found in sheer speed of execution: the work itself could not interest, involving as it did the monotonous repetition of a single process many, many times a day. A high proportion of workers, especially women, most of whom do not expect to spend all their lives in the factory, do not object to this monotony of labour; but it does not follow that it makes for their happiness. A man or a woman can be very unhappy without knowing the cause. Nor is happiness, in the sense of an absence of unhappiness, everything. The countries in which mass-production has advanced furthest profess to be democracies, and expend a great deal of energy on educating their citizens to play an active part in the life of the community. But it is a moot point whether active, democratic citizenship is compatible with working conditions that give the individual no opportunity for creative effort, except in a merely quantitative and money-making sense.

It has, nevertheless, to be recognised that, as long as there are not enough goods and services to allow everyone to live at a reasonable standard, the majority of people will prefer higher productivity to more creative employment. Indeed, in face of the deep poverty of the backward countries, it would be absurd to expect any other opinion to prevail. The backward countries — including not only the most backward, but also a large part of Europe, and of course the Soviet Union — are bound to give pride of place, as far as they are democratically governed, to the task of combating primary poverty by every means in their power. What is disquieting is that in the United States, though a productive level amply sufficient for abolishing poverty has been reached, the first place still appears to be given to more and more production, without any regard for the quality of the labour involved. I am now speaking not of the fact that the United States, with all its growth of productive power, has not abolished poverty within its borders, but of the tendency to multiply wants, and gadgets for satisfying them, and to attach social prestige to gadgetary consumption, without any attempt being made to extend the opportunities for creative endeavour beyond the technicians whose pleasure it is to treat human beings as nearly as possible as if they were machines. No doubt, this concentration on high output has made possible a reduction of hours of labour below the European levels and at the same time a much higher standard of real wages in industry. But the value of more money and of leisure beyond a certain point depends on the possession of means for their real enjoyment; and it is not clear that American happiness is increasing *pari passu* with American productivity. The balance sheet of the good life cannot be drawn up wholly in terms of quantities produced and consumed. This, however, is a matter too large to be settled, or even discussed except cursorily, in this small volume. For most of the world, at any rate, the need to make war on poverty still holds pride of place, and the very changes that are reducing infant mortality and increasing the normal span of human life make this struggle the more pressing, above all for the poorer countries. We must therefore, before attempting to sum up, take a view of the movements of population over the past two centuries and of the population trends which are at work in the world to-day.

XII
Population

Nobody knows what the world's population was two hundred years ago. The best estimates put it at round about 660 millions. A hundred years later it was probably about 1100 millions. In 1951 it is probably approaching 2500 millions. Even now, the total is uncertain, mainly because no one knows the correct figures for China, which is roughly estimated at about 470 millions. We do, however, know that world population has considerably more than doubled during the past hundred years and much more than trebled since 1750.

Two centuries ago, the population of Great Britain was probably about 7½ millions. That of France was three times as great; that of Italy at least twice. Russia may have had 18 millions; Spain, 8 millions; Austria-Hungary, about 7 millions. The territory destined to become the United States had about one million. For Germany as a whole, no figure can be given: Prussia had about 4 millions at most. What the populations of India and China may have been no one even pretends to guess. To-day, Great Britain has about 50 million people, whereas France has only 42 millions. Italy has about 46 millions: Spain, only 28 millions. Western Germany has 48 millions, and Eastern Germany about 18 millions. The United States has over 150 millions, and the Soviet Union is approaching 200 millions. India has roughly 350 millions, and Pakistan another 75 millions: China has more than 450 millions, and Japan about 83 millions. Two hundred years ago, France was easily the most populous of the economically advanced countries: to-day, the United States and the Soviet Union head the list, the one with three and the other with four times as many inhabitants as Great Britain, and both — especially the Soviet Union — with a much greater rate of increase.

How did the world's population come to increase at this prodigious pace? Evidently it could not have done so unless there had been a parallel increase in the supply of foodstuffs; for production at the eighteenth-century level left little or no margin for feeding increased numbers. At the end of that century, Malthus, by way of pouring cold water on the millennial hopes of William Godwin and other believers in the perfectibility of human societies, was prophesying disaster as a consequence of the tendency for population to outrun the means of keeping it alive. Malthus's prophecies were falsified in the nineteenth century by a vast increase in the world's cultivated area, together with a great advance in agricultural productivity in the countries affected by technical progress. In these countries much more food was produced, both because more land was brought into use and because the arts of agriculture and stock-breeding made great advances; and in a few — notably in Great Britain — the home-grown supply of foodstuffs was supplemented by greatly increased imports from overseas, above all from the New World. But over a large part of the earth's surface there was no corresponding advance in agricultural productivity; and the additional mouths were filled by bringing more land into use and by more intensive cultivation based on still primitive techniques. Where industry developed, there was a continuous movement of workers off the land into other occupations: where it did not, more people crowded on to the land, producing more by using more and more labour and often exhausting the resources of the soil under pressure of immediate needs — above all, by cutting down for fuel the trees on which the maintenance of the fertility of the land depended. Elsewhere, the land was wastefully used for the opposite reason — because it was plentiful, and the cultivators snatched from it the largest possible short-term returns, and then moved on to virgin areas to repeat the process.

It does not, however, follow that, because population could not have increased as it did without a great increase in agricultural production, the latter was the cause of the increase. Indeed, the higher agricultural output can be regarded as mainly a response to the need to keep more people alive. There appears to be no doubt that the principal factor making for the great rise in population was not a higher birth-rate — which may or may not have come into effect — but rather a sharp decline in mortality. Falling death-rates, and particularly falling infant death-rates, were certainly of much greater effect than rising birth-rates in most countries about which we know enough to say anything at all. In the more advanced countries the improvement in the expectation of life was largely due to better medical knowledge, which became a specially important factor in decreasing infant mortality. Even the notoriously insanitary conditions of the growing industrial towns did not suffice to check the growth of population: they were not as lethal as the slums of eighteenth-century towns, or even as the eighteenth-century village. At any rate, the rapid increase of population in the first half of the nineteenth century is an unquestionable fact, not only in Great Britain but also in other countries of Western Europe, as well as in the vast areas that were being opened up for settlement in the New World. During the first half of the nineteenth century the population of England and Wales rose from 9 to 18 millions. Over the same period that of France grew, more slowly, from 28 to 36½ millions. The United

States, meanwhile, increased from 5 to 23 millions, and Eastern Europe, including European Russia, from 60 to 89 millions. Europe as a whole had about 187 million people in 1800, and about 266 millions fifty years later.

There is no doubt that this rate of increase — about one-half of one per cent a year for Europe as a whole — was very much greater than that of the preceding centuries. In the eighteenth century, it was even possible for reputable statisticians, such as Richard Price, to believe that the population of England was falling. Such a view would have been absurd at any time in the nineteenth century. But when it comes to explaining why or how the great increase came about, uncertainty sets in. In the absence or virtual absence of practices of birth control,[1] the only factors likely to have affected fertility are earlier marriages and, possibly, greater optimism based on expanding economic opportunity. These can hardly have been the main operative causes of the increase, which must be attributed mainly to lower mortality. But how far the increased survival rates depended on better medical knowledge and hygiene and how far on a decrease in the incidence of famines, epidemics and war devastations, nobody really knows.

We are left, then, with the sheer fact of the increase, and with the certainty that it was closely related to a higher expectation of life, most of all at birth, but to some extent at later ages. And we know that the additional mouths were somehow fed, and that in the more advanced countries there had been, by the middle of the nineteenth century, some real advance in average standards of living — an advance which became much more marked and rapid after 1850. This increase in agricultural production was, for the world as a whole, and even for the greater part of Europe, a much more important fact than

[1] Except, of course, the "natural" control which existed in some kinds of peasant community.

the more spectacular developments in industry. The larger populations needed more clothing and more of other consumers' goods as well as more food; but food was the primary need, without which they could not have survived at all.

Of course, the additional supplies of foodstuffs could not have been made available where they were needed for the development of industry without greatly improved transport; nor, without this, could much of the land that was brought into use have been opened up. In the more advanced countries, the revolutions in agriculture, in transport, and in industry proceeded side by side, each helping on the others. Road and river improvements, better ports and lighthouses and better ships and improved navigation and pilotage, preceded the development of the canals as these preceded the railways. In industry, water-power made its important contribution before steam-power came into widespread use; and horse-power in the literal sense also made its contribution to the development of improved machines.

Changes in population are not simply a matter of there being more or fewer persons: they involve changes in the composition of the people. Populations may increase either because more babies are being born, and are surviving infancy, than are required to offset non-infant deaths, or because the span of adult life is increasing, or because of immigration exceeding emigration. A rise in births or in survivals beyond infancy increases the number of young people; a rise in the expectation of adult life adds to the number of old people; immigration usually means an increase in the numbers of fairly young adults. Where these factors are acting together, there need not be any marked change in the age-composition of the people as a whole; but in most cases when a country has begun to show a sharp increase in population not due mainly to immigration, the principal factor has been a decline in the infant death-rate, and therewith an increase in the proportion of children in the total. The increase in the expectation of adult life has usually become important at a later stage of economic development, and has tended to coincide with a falling birth-rate : so that two factors have been simultaneously at work reducing the proportion of children and adding to that of elderly persons. It is characteristic of rapidly developing countries in the earlier stages of economic advance to have a high proportion of young inhabitants ; whereas in the most advanced societies the proportion of older people is high and tends to become continually higher.

In any society, there are some who work and some who have to be maintained out of the product of those who work. The size of the " working population " depends on social conventions and not on age-distribution alone. Advancing societies move towards universal school education and gradually raise the ages at which children start earning their livings. This reduces the supply of juvenile labour, and usually reduces it most when the proportion of young people in the total population is already falling. At the other end of the life-scale, the operative factor is the age of retirement from work, which depends partly on health and partly on convention, including, in the most advanced societies, the provision of pensions for elderly persons. Hitherto, the tendency has been in these societies towards earlier retirement ; but the great increase in the numbers of the elderly and the improvement in their average physical condition is now leading to the adoption of measures designed to encourage more old people to remain at work.

A period of rapidly increasing population, followed by one in which the rate of increase slows down rapidly, or population becomes stationary, or even begins to fall, carries with it marked changes in age-composition ; but the relative size of the working population as against the combined total of children and elderly persons who are not at work may not be much affected over long periods. Fewer children may be offset by more old people, leaving the proportion of workers much as before. Indeed, a falling birth-rate may for a time increase the proportion of workers, especially if the age of retirement is rising at the same time.

In the preceding paragraph I have been treating housewives as workers — which most of them emphatically are. They are not, however, so treated in the official statistics of " occupied " persons, as these relate only to occupations whose members are paid for their services. The occupied population in this sense is obviously affected by the proportion of women who are " gainfully employed ". The line is, however, very difficult to draw in predominantly agricultural countries, where women commonly share in the work of the farm or peasant holding. In societies which are largely industrial, customs differ about married women going out to work. This is partly a matter of opportunity: for example, in Great Britain the proportion of married women in " gainful employment " has varied widely from area to area. It has been highest in the textile districts, and lowest in the coalfields and in districts mainly devoted to the heavy industries, in which few women are employed.

The Industrial Revolution, in its earlier stages, brought with it a big increase in the numbers of women in factory employment. The textile industries were the first to go over on a large scale to large-scale production with the aid of power-driven machinery; and these industries made very extensive use of the labour of women and children, which had the attraction of cheapness and docility. In effect, this factory employment replaced the employment of women and children in their own homes or in small workshops under the domestic system; but it added to the numbers of full-time wage-earners.

As against this, where, as in some backward areas, industrial development has taken the form mainly of mining or plantation agriculture — which is akin to industry in that it involves large-scale employment — the demand has been chiefly for male labour, with highly adverse effects on the family and tribal structures of the peoples involved — for example, in the Rhodesian copper belt or in Malaya.

As countries become economically more advanced, the proportion of their inhabitants engaged in agriculture usually falls. Mining and manufacture increase their claims on the supply of man-power; and before long transport also usually absorbs a larger percentage of the employed. Then comes a further stage, when there is a rapid rise in employment in what are called "tertiary" occupations — especially distribution and the various forms of clerical and professional employment. A complicating factor here is the employment in domestic service. This is very small in peasant societies, where the domestic work is done mainly by members of the peasant household who also share in other work; but it may be very large where feudal landholding is prevalent and the wealthy classes keep great numbers of family retainers. The growth of industry usually goes, in such areas, with a diminution in the numbers of servants in feudal households; but it usually carries with it a continuous increase in the numbers of servants employed in middle-class families. At a later stage of economic development, the proportions employed in private domestic service may decline, especially if there is a strong demand for labour at rising wages in other occupations; but this decline will be partly offset by the employment of rapidly increasing numbers of domestic workers in hotels, restaurants and institutions of various kinds.

A broad generalisation can safely be made. As societies advance in wealth, there will be relatively fewer agricultural workers and relatively more in " tertiary " occupations. The proportion engaged in manufacture and mining will first rise and then become stationary and still later begin to fall. This is the case even where a country continues to rely on agriculture as its principal source of wealth ; for advanced countries cannot be mainly agricultural unless they carry on their agriculture at a high level of productivity, using relatively little labour except in the production of highly specialised and valuable products. Agriculture has nowhere yielded a high standard of living to those who work in it except when it has become highly mechanised or concentrated on the growing of quality products.

Over the past two centuries, the immense growth of population has been accompanied by a great diversification of jobs. As the Industrial Revolution advanced, it was widely prophesied that the effect of increasing mechanisation would be to destroy the demand for human skill and to reduce men more and more to a dead level of unskilled labour. It was indeed the case that, especially in the textile industries, there was a great destruction of old skills, accompanied, as we saw, by a rapid increase in the employment of women and children as machine-minders. But this was a passing phase — one which has been reproduced in the earlier stages of industrialisation in such countries as Japan and India. In Europe and in the United States, the development of machine-production soon began to require new skills, based on the machine. The machine-makers came to constitute big new groups of skilled workers ; and many of the new machines were found to need highly skilled operation. At the same time, there was an increasing call for kinds of machine dexterity which did not demand either long training or special qualities of intelligence ; and this need for semi-skilled, or merely dexterous, labour increased faster than the demand either for highly skilled or for quite unskilled workers as the modern techniques of mass-production began to develop apace. There was also a rapidly growing demand for clerks, book-keepers, salesmen, technicians and professional workers with their skilled assistants. The total result was by no means an increase in the proportion of what Marx called "undifferentiated human labour". The occupational and social structure of the industrial populations of the advanced countries became increasingly complex: the "middle classes" — meaning those between the capitalist employers and the manual workers — increased fastest of all.

In any society, education, whatever its other uses, must play the part of preparing the people for their work in life. It must turn out, from homes, schools and colleges, the recruits who will be able to fit into the jobs they will find needing to be filled. In some societies, the learning of a skilled job is done mainly by way of apprenticeship, whereas in the more advanced societies much more of it tends to be done in special schools or institutes. The less skilled jobs in all societies are left to be picked up, with or without some kind of "in-training", as it is now called, at the place of work; but in the more advanced societies there is an increasing amount of schooling before "gainful employment" is allowed to begin.

Because the nineteenth century was a period of very rapidly rising population, the classes which had control of the developing means of production were seldom at a loss to find workers to man the increasing array of machines — the more so, because there was a continual movement of population from the rural to the industrial districts. These conditions made it possible to treat labour as a mere commodity which could be bought as easily as the raw materials, the fuel, and the machines needed for production — and indeed more easily, because the labourers had to find work or starve. This plentifulness of human labour helps to account for the inhumanity of the conditions of employment in the earlier phases of the Industrial Revolution in Europe — and later in the more backward countries in which industries were started on the model of those in the more developed areas. On the whole, during the nineteenth century, industrial development took place under conditions in which both labour and capital were plentiful — labour because of the increase of population and the migration of workers from the country to the towns, and capital because the lowness of wages consequent on the abundant supply of labour made possible a high rate of accumulation by the possessing classes.

These conditions, however, did not exist in the United States, where abundant supplies of land and of other natural resources existed, but industrial labour was scarce despite large-scale immigration as long as there was plenty of free land available for settlement. Capital, too, remained scarce for a long time, and local capital had to be eked out, right up to 1914, by borrowing from abroad. Under these circumstances, industrial labour, even without trade union support, was able to strike a better bargain than in the countries of Europe; and even the vast inflow of immigrants during the later years of the nineteenth and the early years of the twentieth century did not suffice to cancel this advantage — though a sharp difference in standards of living arose between the skilled workers and the immigrants from Southern and Eastern Europe who entered the less skilled occupations. The relative scarcity of labour during the formative period of American capitalism was a most important factor in stimulating mechanisation, wherever it could be used to economise on man-power. High American standards of living in the more advanced parts of the United States came much less as a consequence of trade union bargaining than as the effect of labour scarcity and of the high productivity which this scarcity helped to bring about through the use of a high proportion of capital resources. It was, however, never possible to generalise rightly about the whole area of the United States, within which widely different standards of living continued to prevail even among the white population. It needed two wars to bring about even the beginnings of a common standard of living among the American workers; and even to-day the process of assimilation has still a very long way to go.

Nevertheless, the broad contrast between Europe and the United States remains. In the old developed countries in which the new techniques of production were applied, and also in those less developed countries in which an industrial sector was added to a predominantly peasant economy, abundant supplies of labour for a long time kept down working-class standards of living and made possible a rapid advance of capitalist industry that could afford to be wasteful in its use of labour power. As against this, both in the United States and in Canada, Australia and New Zealand, labour, being a scarce factor of production, was able to exact better terms of employment, at any rate for skilled workers; and in consequence more attempt was made to economise in the use of the human factor both in industry and in agriculture.

There is, however, a considerable difference between such countries as Australia, in which the total population remains relatively small, and the United States, with its vast home market and its wide diversity of natural resources. In the United States the home population is big enough to allow mass-production to be carried to great lengths for a very wide range of commodities, even without the necessity of a large export trade. In Australia, on the other hand, the home market is too small to provide an outlet for large-scale production of more than a few things and the high cost of labour stands in the way of building up an export market. Australia exports mainly primary products — wheat, meat and wool — and imports a high proportion of both capital and consumers' goods. This is consistent with a high standard of living because the country has great natural advantages for agricultural production, and has developed these advantages so as to combine an extensive use of land with a limited use of labour. The United States, too, uses land extensively and achieves a high productivity in agriculture for each person employed; and United States exports continue to consist largely of primary products — especially tobacco and cotton. But the United States is also a considerable exporter, despite high wages, of industrial products — above all, of specialised machinery, motor cars, and other products of the metal and engineering industries. In return for its exports it wants mainly raw materials to supplement its domestic supplies; for it can, in the main, supply its consumers' needs out of the products of its own industries. The Americans have been using up their own rich resources of raw materials at a prodigious rate, and have been making larger and larger demands on the resources of other countries. Immediately, this is an advantage to the rest of the world; for it provides dollars with which the sellers of the materials can buy capital goods and consumers' goods from the United States. But already there is danger that the rapid increase of American demand may exhaust the supplies of certain essential materials or, short of that, force up their prices to levels which seriously upset the economic position of less wealthy countries. Moreover, the nature of American trade leaves the whole world unduly vulnerable to fluctuations in American demand. A recession in the United States, by reducing American purchases sharply, cuts off the supply of dollars on which other countries depend for necessary purchases of "dollar" goods, whereas a rate of economic advance exceeding that achieved in other countries makes it difficult for them to get the supplies on which the maintenance of their own levels of employment and prosperity depend.

In effect, if for the moment we leave aside the growth of the Soviet Union, the most significant development of the present century in the economic field has been the increasing domination of most of the world by influences radiating from the United States. The leadership in world economic affairs, which through most of the nineteenth century lay with Great Britain, passed to the United States after the First World War. There was a radical difference between the characters of these two leaderships. In Great Britain after the Industrial Revolution there was a high degree of concentration on export markets, both for consumers' goods, such as cotton and woollen cloth, and, rather later, for capital goods, especially railway material and other products of the metal and engineering trades. In exchange for these goods, Great Britain, as it grew more populous, bought more and more foodstuffs as well as raw materials from abroad, but had also a considerable surplus for foreign lending. British agriculture had its protection withdrawn in order to give the benefit of cheap imports ; and British industry was able to develop large-scale production for the world market to far higher levels than would have been possible for home consumption alone. It is true that one raw material — coal — played as the century advanced an increasing part in the total of British exports ; but in the main Great Britain sent abroad manufactured goods and took in return an unrestricted inflow of foodstuffs and of a wide range of materials not available in sufficient quantities, or not found at all, within the country.

The United States, on the other hand, developed its industries primarily for its vast and rapidly growing home market, which also provided the main outlet for its capital goods. The Americans had what appeared until recently to be abundant home resources of most materials — tin and rubber being the principal exceptions. The need to export affected mainly the agriculturists: the main body of American industrialists took little interest in foreign sales. The rest of the world was much less able to do without goods from America than the Americans were to dispense with imports from the rest of the world. Consequently there developed a tendency for other countries not to acquire enough dollars to pay for what they needed from the United States. In the nineteenth century, no such "gap" appeared in the relations between Great Britain and the rest of the world, partly because Great Britain was the principal market for foodstuffs as well as for raw materials, but also because British capitalists took the lead in developing many of the less advanced countries and thus filled any breach with loans of capital. The United States capitalists were much less ready to invest overseas, except in special cases, such as oil, where America became a keen competitor in a scramble for world resources. After the Second World War, the "dollar gap" could be bridged only by immense gifts as well as loans from the United States to the exhausted countries of Western Europe; and even so Great Britain and other countries found themselves under the absolute necessity of restricting their dollar purchases within the narrowest practicable limits. A "creditor" nation, such as Great Britain was in the nineteenth century and the United States is to-day, must, if its citizens wish to receive payment on their foreign loans, either import more than it exports or keep up an ever-increasing flow of new loans (or gifts) to provide the means of payment. The Americans have indeed given some sign of recognising this necessity, and have done something to reduce their high tariffs on imports of manufactured goods. But their tariff is still high wherever home producers are afraid of foreign competition in their home market; and, even if the tariffs were greatly reduced, the American consumers would probably continue to satisfy most of their requirements by buying home-produced manufactured goods. Consequently, the economic prosperity of that large part of the world which has cause to depend heavily on the United States is highly precarious. Any recession in America, involving reduced American imports of raw materials, hits the economies of the primary-producing countries and, through them, the industrial countries which depend on sales in their markets; and any sharp rise in American demand, while benefiting the primary producers, creates grave difficulties for the countries which have to compete with the United States for scarce supplies of essential materials.

These conditions hardly apply to the Soviet sector of the world economy, though the Soviet Union and its allies can of course be adversely affected by inability to buy the imports they need. Since 1917 the Soviet Union has been swiftly building up, on a foundation of plentiful man-power and widely diversified natural resources, an economy even nearer to self-sufficiency than that of the United States — for although the Soviet Union trades largely with the countries within its sphere of influence, it does so for the most part as a matter of policy rather than of sheer necessity. The standard of life of the Soviet peoples is still very low, and the supplies of consumers' goods which can be got from such countries as Poland and Czechoslovakia are very welcome as means of supplementing home supplies. Home production of consumers' goods has been kept down because the Soviet Union has deliberately given first priority to rapid and intensive industrial development involving a high rate of national saving and a vast investment in the industries which make capital goods. One motive behind this concentration has been military: unless it had existed the Russians could not possibly have held out against the

Nazis through the onslaught of 1941 and the succeeding years — and could not stand out to-day against the Americans. But it has also had an economic basis : it has rested on the calculation that it is worth while to endure hardship for a period of years in order to catch up the most advanced countries in economic equipment and productive skill.

EPILOGUE

To-day

THE growth of modern civilisation, in its economic aspect, rests on the development of what Marx called the "powers of production" — that is to say, on the increase of men's command over the forces of Nature. The civilisation of which Great Britain constitutes a component group is affected in every element of its life and thought by the knowledge which has accumulated in it over centuries at a continually increasing pace of the means of manipulating the forces of Nature to serve human ends. Over the past two centuries this kind of knowledge has been growing much faster than ever before in human history, until in our own day we are finding ourselves compelled to change our habits faster than we can form them, and to revert to a belief in magic and in miracles under the influence of that very science which was formerly the hard-headed antagonist of such notions. So hot has the pace of man's conquest of knowledge become that the successors of those who used to see in it a sure foundation for optimistic theories of progress have taken fright and have become acutely aware of the ambivalence of scientific achievement. It would need a super-optimist to see the liberation of atomic energy as an unmixed blessing, or to ignore, as so many did at an earlier stage of the march of invention, the awareness that the road to destruction, as well as to Utopia, is paved with scientific discoveries.

Yet even those who are most conscious of the ambivalence of science have no thought of obstructing its advance. Nowadays we take that for granted, with only the reservation that the scientists may some day quite soon blow themselves and the world to pieces in one grand holocaust of human hopes and fears. Nowadays, we expect change — rapid change — whether its effects be to our liking or not. This attitude is new — very new indeed for the great majority of mankind. For many thousands of years, generation after generation of men went on living in the possession of vast potential resources of production which they lacked not only the knowledge to use but even the power to recognise as sources of productive power. There was coal under the earth, and even outcropping on its surface; there were rich mineral deposits of many other kinds. Vast latent powers of fertility existed in the soil, and in the unexploited possibilities of breeding and selection of crops and animals; the powers of steam and electricity were there *in posse*, unknown and unapplied. The potentialities of chemical combination were there: atomic energy existed, but no man knew the means of applying it, in either peace or war. To-day, men have knowledge of these things; and, for good and ill, our civilisation is the outcome of this knowledge.

But, even to-day, how much is still unknown; and of what is known how small a part of the human race has been able to take advantage! The great majority of mankind are still living, in China and India and Africa, not unaffected by the development of science and technology, but unable to make use of it for their own purposes, and still practising the arts of production under essentially primitive conditions. Aeroplanes fly over areas that have never been traversed by a locomotive or a motor car: men eat things out of tins which they lack the power to make, and listen in to the news without having ever seen a newspaper. Even in the developed countries, productive performance lags a long way behind the " know how" of the scientific projectors: even in the United States the primitive survives side by side with the new wizardry of mass-production.

Yet it is in the nature of these powers to expand fast and continuously, as soon as any section of the human race has escaped from the bounds and traditions of a static way of living. One discovery or invention leads to another, in an endless chain of development; and the scientist, even when he is not aiming deliberately, as he is in the applied sciences, at economic achievement, is constantly throwing off new knowledge which comes to be of importance in economic practice. The outstanding difference between modern Western civilisation and every other civilisation that has ever existed on earth is — not indeed that it is dynamic whereas they were static, for human affairs never have been static even when the pace of technological change has been nearest zero, but — that modern industrialised societies by their very momentum have made change their second nature. In their climate of opinion, it is impossible to think of Utopia in terms of static and balanced perfection: the ideal comes to be not an end but a process — a continual movement from one victory to another over the forces of nature. Optimism must rest on the acceptance of the beneficence of the advance of knowledge, for unless it does there is nothing for it to stand upon, and pessimism must take its place. Modern man has been caught up into a vast whirlpool of economic development, which will engulf him unless he can master the forces which threaten society with sheer destruction. In one respect, the capitalist countries do appear to have made a great advance in their ability to control the course of events. Up to the 1930s, it was generally regarded as unavoidable that the capitalist world should alternate between booms and depressions and that there should be "bad" years when millions of workers would be unemployed through no fault of their own, and standards of living would be reduced, not because of any fall in productive power, but simply because something had gone wrong with the mechanism of exchange. Even the Socialists, who denounced this state of affairs and demanded the " right to work " — that is to say, an assumption by the State of the responsibility for maintaining the level of employment — usually held it to be impossible to get rid of unemployment under capitalism and regarded Socialism as the only valid remedy.

Nowadays, however, Keynes and Roosevelt between them have caused these judgments to be revised. It has been demonstrated that public policy, even if it cannot abolish unemployment in capitalist countries, can do much to reduce it and to lessen the violence of economic fluctuations by appropriate monetary and budgetary measures designed to maintain the demand for the products of industry. To be sure, the efficacy of these methods of maintaining " full employment " has not yet been really tested; and it may be that the hopes placed in them have been too high. But at the least it can be said that capitalist countries no longer accept widespread unemployment and economic recession as sheer " acts of God ", or as necessary correctives for keeping the working-classes in order. The very growth of the ideas of social security and of the " Welfare State " involves the attempt to maintain a high level of production and employment in order to meet the cost of these forms of provision.

In this respect, then, something has been done to improve man's control over the forces of economic development, though countries still fight shy of the international manœuvres recommended by the more progressive capitalist economists as necessary for avoiding the danger of world economic crisis. But, if there has been at any rate the beginning of an improvement in this respect, its results in terms of human security have been much more than offset by the growing menace of war on a scale destructive far beyond all precedent. Men have more social security, in the advanced countries — provided there is no war. But they do not *feel* more secure, because the threat of war is constantly present to their minds.

Man, in order to achieve security, must master not only the means of controlling his economic fortunes, but also the means to maintaining the world's peace. This, however, is extraordinarily difficult; for the unprecedentedly rapid advance of the powers of destruction, far from making men less prone to arm themselves to the teeth, leads them to expend more and more of their productive power on efforts to increase their security against one another by heavier and ever more costly armaments. Arms, alas, are unlike most other products of industry, in that there is no satiating the demand for them. The more of them one nation has, the more other nations feel they must have too. Moreover, the effect of intensive arming and counter-arming is to increase the influence of the warlike against the peaceable, and to put power into the hands of professionals who are not averse from giving practical demonstration of the efficiency of their weapons of destruction. American air-power in the Korean war has already accomplished, even without the use of atomic weapons, a work of destruction more thorough and more horrible than that of the Second World War; and the atomic weapons that have so far been held in reserve go much further still in sheer destructive power.

Our two centuries of economic growth have not, then, brought us nearer to security; far from it. They have increased greatly the standards of living in the more advanced countries and have made possible, in these countries, new democratic conceptions of human rights to economic welfare. These are very real gains, though they are still limited to a fraction of the human race and have left a considerable part of it untouched in its primary poverty. They are, however, gains which, even within their limited field of application, may at any moment be swept utterly away by the letting loose of the gigantic forces of destruction which are the other outcome of man's advance in the conquest of natural forces.

Thus, the problem of the twentieth century is not primarily economic, even though the need to extend and develop the revolution in economic techniques confronts mankind as insistently as ever — indeed, much more insistently, now that the old mood of acquiescence in primary poverty has passed away in the " dark " continents as well as in the West. Mankind now needs above all else to solve the political problem, both because failure to solve it means destruction and because, as long as it remains unsolved, it offers an insuperable obstacle to an economic advance at all proportionate to the increase in productive power. The greatest economic task of the coming generation is that of lifting the backward peoples out of their poverty and making them sharers in the power to produce wealth which is at present the monopoly of the few among the nations. The Soviet Union, at the cost of immense sacrifices, has been able to advance some way towards this goal by its own efforts, with almost no help from the rest of the world. But it would be infinitely harder for India or China to emulate this achievement because of their much greater populations and their relatively much smaller resources of cultivable land and materials. The economically backward nations need the help of the more advanced; and the more advanced nations need to help them, if only because there is no other way of giving a creative instead of a destructive turn to world unrest.

The problem is that of finding ways of co-operation between the economically advanced and the economically backward peoples that are consistent with the revolt against imperialism over most of the world. The great foreign investments of the nineteenth and early twentieth centuries were made under the conditions of an expanding capitalism and in pursuit of capitalist profit. The investing capitalists were often backed up by their Governments, which also made investments of their own for the purpose of opening up their colonial territories These investments were for the most part made, not because they were to the advantage of the backward countries — whether they were so or not — but because they served the turn of the capitalists of the developed countries. Some of the investments — for example, the establishment of factory industries in India and Shanghai — raised up new competitors against the industries of the advanced countries. But most of them were directed mainly to the opening up of additional sources of food supply and of raw materials which were needed by the advanced countries for their own purposes. Foreign investment thus resulted mainly in larger exchanges of the manufactures, including capital goods, of the more developed countries for the foodstuffs and raw materials of the areas in which the investment took place. In some areas, already closely settled, the effect was to stimulate native production for export, and the main investment was in transport facilities and in commercial enterprises. But in many areas cultivation of the land took the form of " plantation economy ", with planters from the advanced countries employing native labour, much of which was imported from a distance under contract, as in Malaya and Ceylon. When it was a matter of developing mineral resources in the backward areas, the almost invariable structure was that of a company, controlled by white capitalists, employing large bodies of coloured labour under white supervision, with a minority of white workers receiving salaries very many times larger than the wages of the coloured workers. The great companies operating under this system, and also some of the great commercial companies buying the products of native cultivation, were able to derive very large profits from their exploitation of the cheap labour which they found on the spot or imported under contract; and a very high proportion of their gross receipts was taken out of the country in salaries, pensions, shareholders' profits, and taxes levied by the home Governments of the white investors.

The economies of the backward countries thus came to depend on the markets of the more advanced, and to be affected by every fluctuation in the capitalist world. When demand for their products fell, they felt the full brunt of the decline: when demand was good, a large part of the benefit went, not to the native labourers or cultivators, but to the capitalists of the investing countries. Usually, little or nothing was done to train the native employees for the higher types of work, which were monopolised by white men. In many cases the effect of the incursion of white capitalism was to break up the ways of life of the native peoples; and in some colonial areas poll taxes and hut taxes were deliberately imposed in order to drive natives into the only forms of employment in which they could earn the cash needed for paying these imposts. Only a few of the territories affected were climatically or economically suitable for large-scale permanent settlement by white immigrants. In such areas the worst situation of all arose, because the white minorities, determined to preserve their exclusive superiority, used every device for keeping the native inhabitants in a semi-servile status. In areas unsuitable for permanent white settlement, there was usually somewhat better treatment of the natives; but even there the Government was carried on in the interests of the imperialist country, which usually supported its own capitalists against any "uppishness" on the part of the native peoples.

There were indeed marked differences between the colonial policies of the Great Powers. British colonial development was based on a strict colour-bar, with little attempt to assimilate the culture of the colonial peoples to that of the home country. French colonial policy was much less affected by the colour-bar, but aimed at assimilation of a minority of natives to French standards and tried to use this minority as the ally of the home Government against any native aspirations to freedom or race-equality on a more democratic basis. Dutch colonial policy tolerated a large amount of inter-marriage and resulted in the growth of a considerable population of mixed race claiming to receive the privileges of Europeans and serving largely in the lower grades of the administrative hierarchy. Russian expansion into Asia under the Czars was accompanied by heavy pressure for russification, as well as by considerable settlement of Russians in the vast territories of Central and Northern Asia. Germany and Italy, coming late into the field, found most of the more promising territories already occupied. Italian emigration, until after 1914, set mainly towards North America, Argentina and Tunisia; only after the restrictions on emigration which followed the First World War did the Italians attempt a large-scale settlement of colonists in their North African possessions. German emigration also set largely towards the United States; but there were attempts at colonisation in Africa until Germany lost its colonies in the First World War.

These differences of colonial policy did not, however, affect the general character of the movement, which rested everywhere on the convenience of the imperialist countries and not on considerations of what was best for the peoples of the backward countries. This applies to such countries as China and the Middle East as well as to the colonial possessions of the European Powers. Rivalries between the Great Powers prevented either

China or the Middle East as a whole from coming under the exclusive dominion of any one Power; but this did not prevent their resources from being developed, where they were developed at all, to suit the interests of foreign capitalism rather than those of their own inhabitants.

No doubt, in most cases, the effect of foreign investment on the backward countries was to increase both their productivity and their national income, even after the foreign agencies had taken their toll. But wherever the plantation system or mining enterprise developed, the gains accrued mainly to a limited class of native rulers and merchants, and failed to spread to the main body of the native inhabitants. Indeed, imperialist development usually meant alliance between the white man and the most reactionary elements in the countries that were being opened up. Where the native cultivator was left in possession of his land, and white settlement was impracticable, a larger share of the advantages went to the peasant, even after the white merchant companies had skimmed off a heavy profit. This happened, for example, on the Gold Coast and to some extent in Nigeria. In Malaya, Chinese settlers poured in, and won an increasing place in the rubber industry and in trade in competition with the white companies. In Java, too, plantation and peasant cultivation developed side by side. But, broadly speaking, imperialist rule and foreign investment meant the entire subordination of the native economy and way of life to the convenience of the whites.

As long as the coloured peoples accepted their inferiority and their upper classes saw more advantage in siding with the white men against their own peoples than in resisting white penetration, this system could continue and expand. The growth of democratic sentiment and influence in the imperialist countries even did something to improve the treatment of native peoples, where this could be done without detriment to white interests. But from the moment when the Soviet Union had successfully established itself, the situation began to change. Proclaiming a policy of racial equality within its own empire, the Soviet Union became a centre of anti-imperialist activity all over the world. The Soviet leaders set themselves to stimulate the forces making for colonial revolt, allying themselves with colonial nationalism and using colonial nationalist aspirations as a weapon against the imperialist Powers. The world-wide dislocations caused by the Second World War powerfully reinforced this influence, which went, together with the effects of Japanese occupation of a large part of southern Asia, to undermine the prestige of the white man. Communism, defeated in China in the 1920s, was strong enough after the second war to overthrow the American-supported rule of the Kuomintang. Civil war became endemic in Indo-China: the Dutch were compelled to recognise Indonesia as an independent country; the British had to evacuate India and Burma. In West Africa and in the West Indies, the British Labour Government began to make real advances towards colonial self-government. The French lost Syria: Arab nationalism became an important force throughout the Middle East and began to spread to the French possessions in northern Africa.

By this time the flow of capitalist investment in the backward countries, except in the case of oil, had largely dried up. The European countries, impoverished by war and in difficulties over their balances of payments, could no longer afford to make large overseas investments, though the British Government tried to fill part of the gap by providing special funds for colonial development. The only country whose capitalists were in a position to make big investments abroad was the United States; and, except in the case of oil, the American investor, with plenty of opportunities at home, was shy of venturing his money abroad in a world permeated by deep political as well as economic disturbance. For the Americans who did feel like investing abroad, Latin America looked more promising than the backward countries of Asia and Africa; and the United States Government's great gifts went mainly towards helping the economic recovery of Western Europe, in the hope of building up there sufficient strength to resist the advance of Communism from the east. The World Bank for Economic Development, set up after 1945, was designed mainly to undertake projects deemed to be unlikely to attract private investors; but the terms attached to its loans were exacting, and it neither accomplished much itself in the backward countries nor was able to persuade private investors to come forward. President Truman presently put forward his "Fourth Point", proposing large but undefined assistance towards the economic development of these countries; but no more had come of this by 1951 than the spending of relatively small sums on technical assistance and preliminary exploration of the field.

The plain truth is that the less developed countries are for the most part neither in a position nor willing to accept capital investments on terms acceptable to the lenders: nor are the members of the United States Congress prepared to authorise large gifts except where they can see the prospect of a return in the strengthening of the anti-Communist front. In the main, this condition applies to Government loans as well as to outright gifts. Colonial territories did receive some American help under the Marshall Plan; but, as the "cold war" became more intense after 1947, there was an increasing tendency to divert American aid to military purposes and to give precedence to claims that could be brought under the umbrella of "Western Defence".

What, however, the backward areas need most is neither military aid nor aid with capital projects designed to build up exports of raw materials to the advanced countries of the West, but means of improving their agriculture and transport and of producing more of the types of consumers' goods which are needed by the people. Schemes of irrigation, sometimes combined with electrification, were produced in dozens after 1945; but few of them could be carried out for lack of the means of paying for them. Moreover, in many of the backward countries — above all, in the Middle East — the political conditions were desperately unfavourable. The ruling classes feared the effects of economic development in stirring up revolt among the exploited peoples; and funds intended to promote it were apt to disappear with nothing to show.

The political backwardness and class-oppression characteristic of such countries as Persia and Egypt was naturally very helpful to the Communists, who were able to appeal to the peoples with anti-imperialist slogans and to suggest that nothing would be done until the workers and peasants took matters into their own hands and ousted the foreigners and their own ruling class together. They were able to point out that in most of the backward countries the weight of the Western Powers was continually thrown on the side of the most reactionary elements, because these were the readiest to take measures against Communism and the least hostile to foreign capitalist influence. Even where relatively progressive political policies were being followed, as in some of the British colonies, the nationalist, anti-imperialist slogans of the Communists had a considerable appeal.

No doubt, the solution of these problems ought to be looked for in a concerted plan of development for the backward countries, financed by those countries which enjoy a much higher standard of life, and designed to serve the interests primarily of the backward peoples and not of the more advanced. In the long run, the execution of such a plan would be bound to serve the interests of the givers as well as of the recipients. But the cold war has so far bedevilled all such projects. If the United Nations were, in fact, working together, it would be possible under their auspices to work out schemes that would offer help to the backward countries on terms neither too onerous economically nor offensive to the political susceptibilities of rising nationalism. Even so, there would be great difficulties; but there would be a fair chance of overcoming them. It is, however, only necessary to say this to show clearly how unlikely such a state of affairs is. The United Nations cannot work together: there is a sheer incompatibility of outlook among them, not least in the field of world economic development. For the Russians, the way to this must lie through revolution on the Soviet model, and it is therefore necessary to stir up revolt. For the Americans, on the other hand, revolt has come to mean Communism, and must accordingly be prevented at all costs. Even a relaxation of world tension and a nearer approach to the view that capitalism and Communism must somehow contrive to inhabit the world together would still leave the less developed countries as the arena for an ideological struggle in which the Russians would be backing one side and the Americans the other. This situation may not continue permanently; but it certainly exists to-day.

STATISTICAL APPENDIX

RISE OF POPULATION IN CERTAIN COUNTRIES

Approximate totals (Millions)

	c. 1760	*c.* 1780	*c.* 1800	*c.* 1810	*c.* 1820	*c.* 1830	*c.* 1840
Europe	130	150	175	180	..	215	234
United Kingdom	10·8	12·6	15·7	17·9	21	24·1	26·9
Great Britain	8·3	9·5	10·5	11·9	14·2	16·3	18·7
Ireland	2·5	3	5·2	6	6·8	7·8	8·2
France	21	25·1	27·3	29·1	30·5	32·5	34·2
Germany	..	15	23·2	..	27	29·8	32·8
Austria-Hungary	..	20	..	22	..	30	32·8
Italy	..	13	15	18	19	21·2	22
Spain	9	10·2	10·4	..	11·2	..	..
Russia	19	27	37	40	..	45	63
United States	1·25	3	5·3	7·2	9·7	12·9	17·1
Canada	..	..	0·25	..	0·8	0·9	1·7
Argentine	..	..	..	..	..	..	..
Brazil	..	..	..	..	..	..	..
Australia	..	..	..	..	0·04	..	0·26
New Zealand	..	..	..	..	..	..	..
Union of South Africa							
Total	..	..	..	..	..	..	..
White	..	..	..	..	..	..	..
India (and Pakistan)							
British	..	..	..	..	..	..	159
Total	..	..	..	..	..	..	..
China	150	..	..	..	..	..	300
Japan	..	..	..	..	..	..	..

Note.—These figures, especially the early ones, are some cases hardly more than guesses. They are not follow the areas covered by the States at the time: India includes Burma up to 1910, the areas of after 1918; and that of Germany changes again Russian figures include Asiatic Russia, which grew

. 1850	c. 1860	c. 1870	c. 1880	c. 1890	c. 1900	c. 1910	c. 1920	c. 1930	c. 1940	c. 1950
255	282	293	325	380	310*	339	345	376	399	..
27·5	29·1	31·6	35	38·2	41·5	45·2	42·8	44·8	48·2	50·6
20·9	22·3	26·2	29·8	33·5	37	40·8	41·5	43·6	46·9	49·2
6·6	5·8	5·4	5·2	4·7	4·5	4·4	4·3	4·1	4·3	4·4
35·8	36·7	37	37·6	38·8	39	39·6	39·2	41·8	39·8	41·6
35·5	38·1	41	45·2	49·4	56·4	64·9	60·8	64·1	70·1	66 (1946)
..	34·7	35·9	37·6	41·4	45·5	49·5	..	..	..	..
24	25	26·8	28·5	30·3	32·5	34·7	38	41·2	45	46·3
12·5	15·6	16·8	16·8	17·6	18·6	19·9	21·3	23·6	25·9	28·3
68	75	87	84	92	140	147	130	160	171	193 (1946)
23·2	31·4	38·6	50·2	62·9	76	92	105·7	122·8	131·7	151·7
1·8	3·1	3·6	4·3	4·8	5·6	7·2	8·8	10·4	11·4	13·8
1·2	1·4	1·8	..	4	4·5	7	8·5	11·2	14·6	17·2
..	..	10	12	14·3	17·3	25	30·6	40·3	41·4	52·1
0·5	1·2	1·9	2·7	3·2	3·8	4·5	5·4	6·4	7	8·2
..	0·1	0·3	0·5	0·6	0·8	1	1·2	1·5	1·6	1·9
..	..	..	..	2·75	4·5	6	7·5	8	10·4	12·3
..	..	..	..	0·6	1	1·3	1·5	1·8	2·2	..
178	196	195	199	221	232	244	247	256	295	..
..	..	241	254	287	294	315	319	351	385	422
..	..	390	..	..	..	420	..	444	458	465
27	..	33	36	40	48	54	59·7	64·4	73·1	83·2

* Excluding USSR. from 1900 onwards.

many cases only very rough approximations — in
r uniform territories at the different dates, but
us, United Kingdom includes Eire up to 1920,
ermany and France change after 1871 and again
er 1945. The Chinese figures are guesswork. The
eatly through most of the past century.

RAILWAY DEVELOPMENT FROM 1840: SELECTED COUNTRIES

(Miles of Line open for Traffic)

	1840	1850	1860	1870	1880	1890	1900
United States	2820	9020	30,630	53,400	84,393	161,397	194,26
United Kingdom	838	6620	10,430	15,540	17,935	20,073	21,85
France	360	1890	5,880	9,770	14,500	22,700	25,00
Germany	341	3640	6,980	11,730	20,690	26,750	32,33
Belgium	210	550	1,070	1,800	2,400	2,800	..
Austria-Hungary	90	960	2,810	5,950	11,500	16,000	..
Canada	16	70	2,090	2,500	6,890	13,256	..
Russia	16	310	990	7,100	14,020	18,059	36,50
Italy	13	270	1,120	3,830	5,340	8,090	9,31
Holland	11	110	208	780	1,440	1,570	..
Spain	..	80	1,190	3,200	4,550	6,220	..
Denmark	..	20	70	470	830	1,247	..
Switzerland	..	15	650	890	1,600	1,870	..
India (and Pakistan)	..	..	840	4,830	9,310	16,977	24,75
Sweden	..	..	375	1,090	3,650	5,174	..
Egypt	..	..	275	550	1,120	1,158	..
Australia	..	..	250	1,230	5,390	10,141	..
Brazil	..	..	135	505	2,175	4,700	..
Chile	..	..	120	450	1,100	1,700	..
Peru	..	..	50	250	1,180	880	..
Argentine	..	..	15	640	1,540	5,869	10,304
Mexico	..	..	..	220	660	4,648	..
Turkey	..	..	..	113	1,137 (1876)	1,296	..
Uruguay	..	..	..	60	270	707	..
Union of South Africa	..	..	..	..	1,040	3,355	4,90
Algeria	..	..	..	..	780	1,910	..
Japan	..	..	..	..	75	1,438	3,63
China (including Manchuria)	..	..	..	12 (1876)	..	90	..

Note.—No high degree of accuracy is claimed f
up on a uniform basis; there are problems of i
different ways of measuring track-miles (*e.g.* sing
for the same territories at all dates; and there ha
figures are of more use as measuring broadly t
mileages. They are, for the most part, accura

1905	1910	1920	1930	1940	1950 (or latest available)	
218,291	242,107	253,152	262,213	246,739	238,060	
22,907	23,387	20,312	20,265	19,900	19,600	Eire excluded from 1920.
29,018	25,390	25,167	26,177	26,430	26,430	Excluding local light railways.
34,526	38,747	35,919	36,231	36,684	..	Loss of territory after 1918.
4,375	5,340	5,455	6,093	6,029	6,755	
24,338	27,333	..	..	..	..	Austria-Hungary ceased to be a unity after 1918.
21,280	26,624	39,170	42,075	42,637	42,248	
39,591	45,078	29,909	48,236	59,375	65,824 (1945)	1920 figure affected by war.
10,120	10,570	9,741	13,844	14,334	14,000	1920 figure omits African lines.
2,133	1,994	2,377	2,287	2,105	2,005	
8,782	9,160	9,436	10,138	10,400	8,064	
2,043	2,134	2,662	3,290	3,163	3,049	
2,640	3,154	3,915	3,367	3,660	3,600	
28,221	32,099	37,029	42,281	41,052	40,524*	
7,815	7,812	9,420	10,506	10,486	10,489	
3,233	2,278	3,032	3,358	3,690	3,816	
14,988	16,968	24,263	27,477	27,999	27,076	
10,600	13,611	17,847	19,840	21,380	22,140	
2,939	3,697	5,403	5,540	5,220	5,525	
1,299	1,682	1,984	2,810	3,000	2,581	
12,230	17,380	22,590	25,435	26,840	27,000	
12,227	15,000	11,154	18,119	14,690	13,896	Figures affected by dislocation of railways after 1910.
3,110	3,500	2,160	3,965	4,450	4,770	Change of territory after 1910.
1,210	1,570	1,625	1,729	1,874	1,828	
..	8,091	10,144	12,873	13,238	13,340	
..	2,060	2,221	3,009	..	3,000	
4,693	5,354	8,207	12,821	14,912	..	
3,435	5,820	7,000	14,192	14,000	14,000	Figures only very rough approximations.

* 1950, add 6500 miles Indian State railways.

hese figures. The national statistics are not drawn
lusion or exclusion of light railways, etc., as well as
nd double lines, sidings, etc.). The figures are not
een some changes in classification. In general, the
ates of development than as recording absolute
nough for this purpose.

SOME CITY POPULATIONS, 1831, 1881, 1931 AND ABOUT 1950

(Thousands)

	c. 1831	c. 1881	c. 1931	Latest Available
London	1655	3816	8203	8197 (1947)
Paris	786	2250	2871	2725 (1947)
Istanbul (Constantinople)	590	850	700	850 (1940)
Naples	354	463	850	995 (1947)
Cairo	333	370	1100	1307 (1937)
Leningrad (St. Petersburg)	324	900	2783	3191 (1939)
Moscow	308	750	2800	4137 (1939)
Vienna	280	1104	1886	1951 (1948)
Calcutta	280	871	1486	2707 (1947)
Manchester	238 *	517 *	766	701 (1949)
Bombay	229	773	1161	1698 (1947)
Dublin	227	350	320	528 (1949)
Berlin	220	1300	4000	3190 (1946)
Madrid	205	390	1000	1440 (1949)
New York	203	1200	6930	8067 (1949)
Lisbon	202	250	590	705 (1940)
Amsterdam	201	350	770	837 (1950)
Palermo	168	206	330	497 (1950)
Philadelphia	167	850	1951	1950 (1940)
Liverpool	165	552	856	802 (1949)
Glasgow	164	500	1088	1105 (1949)
Warsaw	151	401	1179	600 (1945)
Rome	128	273	1045	1588 (1947)
Tokyo	..	900	5312	4175 (1947)
Chicago	..	503	3376	3397 (1940)
Birmingham	..	401	1002	1107 (1949)
Budapest	..	400	1000	1058 (1949)
Shanghai	..	388	3200	3600 (1949)
Buenos Aires	..	350	2215	3000 (1947)
Osaka	..	350	2600	1599 (1947)
Rio de Janeiro	..	340	1500	2500 (1948)
Melbourne	..	330	992	1259 (1949)
Mexico City	..	300	970	1468 (1940)
Barcelona	..	260	1100	1269 (1949)
Sydney	..	220	1239	1484 (1947)
Montreal	..	140	1100	1075 (1949)
Detroit	..	80	1570	1623 (1940)
Canton	..	..	1500	870 (1949)
Pekin	..	..	1300	1688 (1949)
Nanking	..	..	1300	807 (1949)
Los Angeles	..	..	1238	1504 (1940)
Hamburg	..	300	1130	1384 (1946)
Milan	..	296	1013	1270 (1947)
São Paulo	..	40	880	1543 (1948)
Prague	..	162	850	944 (1946)

* With Salford.

IMMIGRATION INTO THE UNITED STATES

(Thousands)

	Total	Net Approximate	Total from Europe	Total from Other Sources	Total U.S. Population beginning of Decade	Total from U.K. including Ireland
1821–30	152	100	107	45	9,655	100
1831–40	599	600	496	103	12,866	308
1841–50	1713	1600	1598	115	17,063	1095
1851–60	2598	2500	2453	145	23,192	1317
1861–70	2315	2300	2065	250	31,443	1133
1871–80	2812	2500	2272	540	38,558	1087
1881–90	5247	4300	4737	510	50,156	1714
1891–1900	3688	3200	3559	129	62,481	1091
1901–10	8795	5600	8136	659	75,995	..
1911–20	6347	3100	4377	1359	91,972	..
1921–7	3279	2000	2013	1266	105,711	..

NATIONALITIES OF IMMIGRANTS INTO THE UNITED STATES

A. Nationalities of Persons Immigrating into the United States, 1871–95			B. Countries of Birth of Foreign White Persons in U.S.A., 1940	
	Numbers (Thousands)	% of Total		Numbers (Thousands)
German	2608	25·3	Italy	1624
British	1622	15·7	Germany	1238
Irish	1335	12·9	Russia	1041
Scandinavian	1151	11·1	Poland	993
North American	776	7·5	Great Britain	622
Italian	655	6·3	Eire	572
Russian	501	4·8	Austria	480
Austrian	375	3·6	Sweden	445
Hungarian	256	2·5	Czechoslovakia	320
French	149	1·4	Hungary	290
Polish	142	1·4	Norway	262
Swiss	136	1·3	Greece	163
Czech	77	0·7	Denmark	138
Belgian	42	0·4	Finland	117
Other European	52	0·6	France	103
Others	366	3·8		

DATE LIST

		Inventions and Discoveries, and Capital Works
1751		
1752		Franklin's Lightning Conductor
1753		
1754		Lind's *Treatise on the Scurvy* Black discovers Carbonic Acid Gas
1755		*c.* Huntsman makes Cast Steel
1756		
1757		
1758		
1759		Smeaton's Eddystone Lighthouse
1760		Carron Ironworks
1761	CANAL ERA BEGINS	Bridgewater Canal
1762		Dixon's Experiments with Coal Gas
1763		
1764		Hargreaves's Spinning Jenny
1765		
1766		
1767		Watson distils Coal
1768		Cavendish discovers Hydrogen
1769	STEAM-POWER AND COAL	Watt's Steam-Engine patented
1770	MACHINE SPINNING	Arkwright's Water-Frame Cugnot's Steam Carriage
1771		
1772		Cavendish's Electrical Experiments Whitehurst's Hydraulic Water Ram
1773		Montgolfier's Balloon
1774		Priestley discovers Oxygen
1775		
1776		Watt's first Coal-mine Engine

ECONOMIC DEVELOPMENTS, ETC., FROM 1751

Economic Policy and Organisation	*Political and International Affairs*	*Other Events*
	Clive takes Arcot	First Part of French *Encyclopédie*
Sèvres Porcelain Factory		
Bakewell begins Stock-breeding		
	Seven Years' War begins	
	Clive's Victory at Plassey	
		Quesnay's *Tableau économique*
	British Conquest of Canada	
		Rousseau's *Du contrat social*
	Captain Cook's Voyages (–1779)	First volume of *Encyclopaedia Britannica*
Wedgwood's Etruria Works		
	Russian Conquest of Crimea	
	First Partition of Poland	
	Hastings Governor-General of India	
	AMERICAN DECLARATION OF INDEPENDENCE	Adam Smith's *Wealth of Nations*

		Inventions and Discoveries, and Capital Works
1777		Grand Trunk Canal finished
1778		Lavoisier destroys Phlogiston Theory Bramah's Water-closet
1779		Crompton's Spinning Mule Tar produced from Coal (Dixon) Coalbrookdale Iron Bridge
1780		
1781		
1782		Watt's Double-acting Engine
1783		Hunter founds Museum of Anatomy
1784	COACHING AGE; EXPANSION OF IRON INDUSTRY	Cort's Puddling Process Murdoch's Steam Carriage Argand Oil Lamp
1785		Cartwright's Power-Loom Berthollet's Bleaching Process
1786		First Threshing Machines
1787		
1788		
1789		Lavoisier lists Chemical Elements Electrical Controversy of Galvani and Volta
1790		Leblanc's Soda Process Cartwright's Wool-combing Machine Rotary Printing Press
1791		
1792		Murdoch's Gas Lighting Apparatus
1793	AGRICULTURAL ENCLOSURE INCREASES	Chappe's Aerial Telegraph
1794		Maudsley's Slide Rest Whitney's Cotton Gin
1795		*c.* Jacquard's Loom
1796		Jenner begins Inoculation Senefelder's Lithographic Presses
1797		

Economic Policy and Organisation	*Political and International Affairs*	*Other Events*
Bath and West Agricultural Society		
Coke of Norfolk begins farming		
c. Rapid Increase in Coal Output		
Creusot Works started		
Palmer organises Mail Coaches		
	U.S. Constitution drawn up (in force 1789)	
	Settlement of New South Wales	
	French Revolution	Buffon's *Natural History* completed
		Declaration of the Rights of Man
		Burke's *Reflections on the French Revolution*
		Paine's *Rights of Man*
British Board of Agriculture	Britain and France at War	Godwin's *Political Justice*
	Second Partition of Poland	
British Canal Mania (–1797)	French abolish Slavery	
	English Treason Trials	
Speenhamland System introduced	Third Partition of Poland	
Bank of England suspends Gold Payments		

DATE LIST—*continued*

		Inventions and Discoveries, and Capital Works
1798		Curr's Rope-hoisting Improvements in Mines
1799		Royal Institution
1800		Volta's Pile Herschel discovers Infra-red Rays
1801		First British Census
1802	STEAMSHIPS	Symington's *Charlotte Dundas* West India Dock opened
1803	POWER WEAVING SPREADS	Horrocks's Power-Loom Steam Threshing Machine
1804		Trevithick's Steam Carriage
1805		Telford's Pont Cysylte Aqueduct
1806		Davy discovers Potassium and Sodium
1807		Fulton's *Clermont* Sommering's Electric Telegraph
1808		Dalton formulates Atomic Theory Gay-Lussac's work on Gases
1809		
1810		Davy isolates Chlorine *c.* Cast Iron Water Pipes introduced
1811	LOCOMOTIVES	Hackworth's *Puffing Billy* Koenig's Power Printing Press
1812		Bell's *Comet* Blenkinsop's Locomotive
1813		
1814		Stephenson's first Locomotives *The Times* printed by machinery
1815		Davy's Safety Lamp Telford's Holyhead Road begun
1816		Brewster's Kaleidoscope
1817		Clegg's Gasometer
1818		
1819		*Savannah* crosses Atlantic Oersted's Electro-magnetic Discoveries

Economic Policy and Organisation	*Political and International Affairs*	*Other Events*
Smithfield Club Pitt's Income Tax	Irish Rebellion	Malthus's *Essay on Population*
Combination Act	Napoleon First Consul	
Bank of France Owen acquires New Lanark		
British General Enclosure Act		
	Louisiana Purchase	
Public Gas Lighting begins (Windsor)		*Code Napoléon* (–1810)
Berlin Decrees	Britain ends Slave Trade	
Orders in Council		
Lancasterian Association		
Luddite Troubles (–1811)	Revolt of Latin America begins	
	British-American War (–1815)	
Repeal of Statute of Artificers (–1814)	East India Co. loses Monopoly	Owen's *New View of Society*
British Corn Law	End of French Wars	
		Ricardo's *Political Economy*
Institution of Civil Engineers established		Cuvier's *Animal Kingdom*
First British Factory Act Peterloo Massacre: Six Acts	U.S. purchases Florida Singapore founded	

		Inventions and Discoveries, and Capital Works
1820		*c.* Ampère's work on Electrodynamics
1821		Faraday discovers Electromagnetic Rotation
1822		Babbage's first Calculating Machine Church's Type-casting Machine
1823	CHEMICAL INDUSTRY EXPANDS	Faraday liquefies Chlorine Simpson's Sand Water Filter Muspratt's Alkali Works
1824		*c.* Maudsley's Improved Lathes
1825		Roberts's Self-acting Mule Erie Canal finished Brunel's Thames Tunnel begun
1826	RAILWAY AGE BEGINS	Stockton and Darlington Railway Telford's Menai Bridge finished Krupp begins Arms Production Ohm's Law formulated
1827		Bell's Reaping Machine
1828	IRON INDUSTRY DEVELOPS	Neilson's Hot Blast Dunforth's Ring-spinning Machine
1829		Rainhill Trials : Stephenson's *Rocket*
1830		Thimonier's Sewing Machine
1831		*c.* Faraday's Electrical Discoveries
1832		
1833		Weber and Gauss's Electric Telegraph Whitworth begins work on Standardisation
1834		McCormick's Reaping Machine Hall's Cage for Hoisting in Mines
1835		Jacobi's Electric Motor Geological Survey instituted
1836		Ericsson's Screw-Propeller

Economic Policy and Organisation	*Political and International Affairs*	*Other Events*
Bank of England resumes Gold Payments		
	Greek War of Independence	Owen's *Report to the County of Lanark*
Belgian *Société Générale*		
	Irish Catholic Association Monroe Doctrine Britain recognises Latin American Republics	
British Combination Acts repealed Commercial Crisis		Saint-Simon's *Catéchisme des industriels*
	Catholic Emancipation Act	
British Agricultural Labourers' Revolt	French and Belgian Revolutions Polish Insurrection	Comte's *Philosophie positive* (vol. i)
First British Cholera Epidemic British Association founded	Young Italy Party	
	British Reform Act	
Grand National Consolidated Trades Union First State Grant for Education (Britain)		
British Poor Law Act German *Zollverein*		
British Highways Act		
British Newspaper Duties reduced First Railway Boom		

		Inventions and Discoveries, and Capital Works
1837	TELEGRAPHY	Cooke and Wheatstone's Electric Telegraph Railway open from London to Manchester
1838		*Sirius* and *Great Western* cross Atlantic by steam
1839		Nasmyth's Steam Hammer Daguerre's Photographic Process
1840	SHIPPING LINES	Rothamsted established *c.* Electrotyping introduced
1841		Fox Talbot's Photographic Process Whitworth's Standard Screw Threads Clark's Water-Softening Process
1842		Lawes's Superphosphate Patent
1843		
1844		Morse's Telegraph
1845		Schonbein makes Celluloid Armstrong's Hydraulic Crane
1846		Hoe's Revolving Printing Machine
1847		
1848		
1849		Reuter's founded
1850	SPREAD OF IRON SHIP	Stephenson's Menai Bridge finished Singer's Sewing Machine
1851		Submarine Telegraph (Dover–Calais) *c.* Mechanical Ventilation in Mines begins
1852		Giffard's Steam Airship
1853		Brunel's Saltash Bridge
1854		

Economic Policy and Organisation	*Political and International Affairs*	*Other Events*
Royal Agricultural Society		*The People's Charter*
Anti-Corn Law League	First Chartist Petition Chinese Opium War	L. Blanc's *Organisation du travail*
Penny Post in Britain Cunard Line		
	Hong Kong ceded to Britain	
Peel reduces British Tariff Income Tax reimposed	French Conquest of Algeria (–1847) Second Chartist Petition	Chadwick's *Report on the Sanitary Condition of the Labouring Population*
Period of Railway Consolidation begins British Bank Charter Act Rochdale Pioneers		
Chartist Land Scheme	U.S. annexes Texas	
British Corn Laws repealed Ten Hours Act	Oregon Boundary Settlement	
Second Cholera Epidemic Californian Gold Discoveries	Year of Revolutions in Europe Third Chartist Petition	Mill's *Principles of Political Economy* Marx's *Communist Manifesto*
British Navigation Acts repealed	Britain annexes Punjab	
Great Exhibition Australian Gold Discoveries	Napoleon's *Coup d'État*	
British Industrial and Provident Societies Act		
	Perry opens Japan to Trade	
	Crimean War (–1856)	

		Inventions and Discoveries, and Capital Works
1855		
1856	STEEL INDUSTRY DEVELOPS	Bessemer's Converter
1857		First Attempt to lay Atlantic Cable Nollet's Magneto-Dynamo for Light-houses Perkin's Aniline Dyes Mushet's Alloy Steel
1858		*Great Eastern* launched
1859	RISE OF OIL INDUSTRY BEGINS	First Oil Well dug in U.S.
1860		Pacinotti's Ring-wound Armature
1861		Graham's Colloid Experiments Massachusetts Institute of Technology
1862		Parkes's first Plastics
1863		Ridley and Jones's Mechanical Pick
1864		Clark Maxwell's Equations
1865		Lister begins Antiseptic Surgery Hughes's Printing Telegraph Solvay's Sodium Process
1866	GROWTH OF GERMAN INDUSTRY	Siemens's Open Hearth Process Atlantic Cable laid by *Great Eastern* Mendel publishes his Researches
1867		Martin uses Scrap for Open Hearth Process Ferro-manganese Steel introduced
1868		Walter's Rotary Printing Machine
1869		Suez Canal opened Central Pacific Railway opened Collotype Process
1870	GROWTH OF AMERICAN WHEAT EXPORTS	Pasteur's work on Silkworms Gamme's Electric Dynamo
1871		Montcenis Tunnel opened Ingersoll's Pneumatic Drill

Economic Policy and Organisation	*Political and International Affairs*	*Other Events*
British Newspaper Duties abolished British Limited Liability Act	Second Opium War	
	Indian Mutiny	
		Darwin's *Origin of Species* Liebig's *Letters on Agriculture*
Gladstone's Free Trade Budget : Cobden Treaty		
Lancashire Cotton Famine begins	Serfdom abolished in Russia American Civil War (–1865)	
U.S. Homestead Act British Companies Act	France annexes Cochin China	
English Co-operative Wholesale Society	Emancipation proclaimed in U.S.	
	International Working-Men's Association	
Latin Monetary Union	Irish Fenian Movement	
Overend and Gurney Crisis	Austro-Prussian War	
	Second British Reform Act Alaska Purchase Dominion of Canada	Marx's *Capital*
British Trades Union Congress		Dilke's *Greater Britain*
British Education Act British Civil Service reformed	Franco-Prussian War Unification of Italy	
British Trade Union Act	Paris Commune Japan abolishes Feudalism German Empire established	

		Inventions and Discoveries, and Capital Works
1872		Photo-reproduction of Line Drawings begins Edison's Duplex Telegraphy
1873	RISE OF CHEMICAL INDUSTRY	First Effective Typewriter Mond sets up Winnington Chemical Works
1874		Refrigerated Meat Trade begins
1875	"GREAT DEPRESSION" BEGINS	
1876		Bell's Telephone Edison's Phonograph
1877		Otto's Gas Engine
1878		Brush's Arc Light Hughes's Microphone Kelvin's Improved Mariner's Compass Gilchrist Thomas's Basic Steel Process
1879		First Steel Merchant Ships built
1880	RISE OF ELECTRICAL INDUSTRIES	Swan's and Edison's Electric Lamps
1881		Paris Exhibition lighted by Electricity Brush's and Edison's Dynamos Pasteur's Demonstration of Vaccination Construction of Vyrnwy Dam begins Goubet's Submarine
1882	PARTITION OF AFRICA BEGINS	Meisenbach's Half-tone Process
1883		Tesla's Alternating Current Motor Maxim's Machine Gun
1884	RISE IN GOLD OUTPUT	Parsons's Steam Turbine
1885		Mergenthaler's Linotype Machine Canadian Pacific Railway finished
1886		Daimler's Petrol Engine
1887		Berliner's Gramophone Cyanide Process of Extracting Gold

Economic Policy and Organisation	Political and International Affairs	Other Events
Germany adopts Gold Standard		
irst Shipping " Conference "	German Socialist Party unified	
Universal Postal Union		
	Bulgarian Atrocities	
	Victoria proclaimed Empress of India	
	Leopold's Congo International Association	
Telephone Companies founded	Treaty of Berlin	
	Bismarck's Anti-Socialist Laws	
Germany nationalises Railways	Irish Land League	George's *Progress and Poverty*
ritish Agricultural Crisis		
	Increased Immigration to U.S.	
rance starts Shipping Subsidies	France occupies Tunis	
	British North Borneo Co.	
	Royal Niger Co.	
tandard Oil Co. founded	Triple Alliance	
ismarck's Social Insurance Laws		
Witwatersrand Goldfield discovered	Germany acquires South-West Africa	
	Third British Reform Act	
	British Conquest of Nigeria (–1886)	
Germany and U.S. adopt Shipping Subsidies	Gordon dies at Khartoum	
Transvaal Gold Rush	Gladstone's Irish Home Rule Proposals	
	First British Colonial Conference	

		Inventions and Discoveries, and Capital Works
1888		Ferranti's Deptford Power Station Hertz's Work on Western Telegraphy Pasteur Institute
1889		Friese-Greene's Cinematographic Patent
1890		First Turbine-driven Power Station (Forth Banks) *c.* Lanston's Monotype Machine
1891		Electric Trams begin City and South London Tube Trans-Siberian Railway begun
1892		
1893		
1894		Marconi's First Radio Experiments Manchester Ship Canal finished
1895		Film Projection begins Electric Railways begin Kiel Canal opened
1896		Röntgen discovers X-rays Northcliffe's *Daily Mail*
1897		
1898		
1899		Mme Curie discovers Radium London School of Tropical Medicine
1900		Zeppelin's first Airship
1901	RADIO AGE BEGINS	Marconi radios across Atlantic
1902		National Physical Laboratory
1903	MOTORING AGE BEGINS	Ford Motor Co. founded Wright Brothers' Aeroplane First Diesel Ships

Economic Policy and Organisation	*Political and International Affairs*	*Other Events*
	British East Africa Co.	
ondon Dock Strike	British South Africa Co. Brazilian Republic	*Fabian Essays*
oyal Dutch Oil Co.	McKinley Tariff (U.S.) Sherman Anti-Trust Law (U.S.)	Marshall's *Principles of Economics*
	Franco-Russian Alliance	
henish-Westphalia Coal Syndicate	British I.L.P. founded	
	Sino-Japanese War Dreyfus Case Armenian Massacres (–1896)	
onfédération Générale du Travail	Japan acquires Formosa France annexes Madagascar Jameson Raid	
londyke Gold Rush		
ingley Tariff (U.S.)	Canada begins Imperial Preference Germany occupies Kiaochow	
mperial Penny Postage	Fashoda Incident Spanish-American War Russian Lease of Port Arthur	
ritish Colonial Railway Development begins	South African War (–1901) U.S. announces Open Door in China	
ritish Colonial Stock Act	Boxer Rebellion in China British Labour Party founded International Socialist Bureau	
.S. Steel Corporation	Commonwealth of Australia	
erman Tariff raised	Anglo-Japanese Alliance	
hamberlain's Tariff Reform Campaign	South Africa and New Zealand adopt Imperial Preference Republic of Panama Increased Immigration to Argentine	

		Inventions and Discoveries, and Capital Works
1904		Fleming's Valve (Wireless)
1905	CINEMA AGE BEGINS	Einstein's Special Theory of Relativity First Cinemas opened Rubel's Offset Process
1906		Fleming's Valve improved by De Forest
1907		Bakelund's Work on Plastics
1908		
1909	AEROPLANE AGE BEGINS	Ford builds first Tractors Blériot flies the Channel
1910		First Motor Tanker built *c.* Poulsen's Arc Generator for Wireless Telegraphy
1911		
1912		
1913		
1914	FIRST WORLD WAR	Panama Canal opened
1915		First Tanks built
1916		Einstein's General Theory of Relativity Synthetic Rubber produced in Germany
1917	RUSSIAN REVOLUTION: RISE OF COMMUNISM	
1918		
1919		Alcock and Brown fly the Atlantic

Economic Policy and Organisation	*Political and International Affairs*	*Other Events*
	Entente Cordiale Russo-Japanese War	
	First Russian Revolution	
British Trade Disputes Act	Liberal Victory in Britain	
Royal Dutch–Shell Oil Combine U.S. Financial Crisis	Dominion of New Zealand	
British Old Age Pensions Act	Australia adopts Imperial Preference Young Turk Revolution	
Anglo-Persian Oil Co. Lloyd George's Budget	Wave of Immigration to U.S.	
	Union of South Africa Japan annexes Korea	
Labour Unrest in Britain (–1914)	Agadir Crisis Italian Annexations in North Africa	
	Chinese Republic First Balkan War French Protectorate in Morocco	
Federal Reserve Banking System (U.S.) Clayton Anti-Trust Law (U.S.)	First World War (–1918)	
British Shop Stewards' Movement begins	Japan's "21 Demands" on China	
British Department of Scientific and Industrial Research	Irish Rebellion	
	Russian Revolution U.S. enters War India puts Taxes on Imported Cottons Balfour Declaration of Jewish National Home Brest-Litovsk Treaty German Revolution	Lenin's *State and Revolution*
British Coal Commission Washington Conference (I.L.O.)	Versailles Treaty: League of Nations Third International Amritsar Massacre	

		Inventions and Discoveries, and Capital Works
1920	ATOMIC RESEARCH SUCCEEDS	British Medical Research Council Rutherford splits the Atom
1921	RADIO AGE BEGINS	Broadcasting begins in U.S.
1922		British Broadcasting begins
1923		
1924		First Radar Experiments (Appleton)
1925		Short-wave Beam Wireless begins
1926		Baird's Television Demonstrations
1927		First Talking Films De la Cierva's *Autogyro* British Electricity Grid begun
1928		Fleming discovers Penicillin
1929		
1930		
1931	WORLD ECONOMIC CRISIS	
1932		
1933	NAZI REVOLUTION	
1934		
1935		Radar applied to Aircraft Location Gas Turbine Engine comes into use Iraq Pipe-line finished Sulphonamide Drugs introduced
1936		Television Broadcasting begins
1937		

Economic Policy and Organisation	Political and International Affairs	Other Events
Russian Electrification Plan	Russo-Polish War Prohibition in U.S. Irish Civil War	
Post-war Slump begins New Economic Policy in Russia	Irish Treaty	
	Fascist *coup* in Italy Italian Conquests in Africa resumed	
	French occupy Ruhr Dictatorship in Spain	
Dawes Reparations Plan	Kemal President of Turkey U.S. Immigration Act	
Britain restores Gold Standard	Locarno Pact	
Continental Steel Cartel British General Strike	Kuomintang Victory in China	
	Kuomintang expels Communists	
First Russian Five-Year Plan		
Depression begins in U.S. Collectivisation of Russian Agriculture begins	Indian Congress demands Independence	
Hawley-Smoot Tariff (U.S.) Young Reparations Plan	Indian Round Table Conferences (–1933) London Naval Conference	
Britain leaves Gold Standard	Japan invades Manchuria	
Ottawa Tariff Conference Suicide of Ivar Kreuger	Disarmament Conference	
Roosevelt's New Deal World Economic Conference	Nazi Revolution in Germany	
	Austrian Socialists suppressed Kirov assassinated Abyssinian Crisis	
	Nazis occupy Rhineland Spanish Civil War	Keynes's *General Theory of Employment*
	Front Populaire in France Japan invades China	

DATE LIST—*continued*

		Inventions and Discoveries, and Capital Works
1938		
1939	SECOND WORLD WAR	
1940		
1941		Whittle's Jet Engine
1942		
1943		
1944		German Flying Bombs
1945	FIRST ATOMIC BOMBS	
1946		
1947	"COLD WAR" BEGINS	Guided Rocket Missiles made
1948		Synchro-cyclotron constructed
1949		
1950		U.S. authorises production of Hydrogen Bomb
1951		

Economic Policy and Organisation	*Political and International Affairs*	*Other Events*
	Nazis occupy Austria Munich Crisis	
	Second World War (–1945)	
	Fall of France	
	Nazis invade Russia U.S. enters War Atlantic Charter	
Bretton Woods Conference	D-Day Dumbarton Oaks Conference	
	World War ends Labour Government in Britain United Nations Charter	
U.S. Loan to Britain		
Marshall Plan announced Geneva Trade Conference	India and Pakistan Dominions Cominform set up	
	Communist *coup* in Czechoslovakia State of Israel established Yugoslav break with Cominform	
Truman's " Point Four " Development Programme	Communist Victory in China	
Schuman Plan formulated	Korean War begins Colombo Conference on South-East Asia Persian Oil Crisis Egypt denounces Treaty with Britain	

INDEX

Index

Index

THE END

PRINTED BY R. & R. CLARK, LTD., EDINBURGH